CHICAGO PUBLIC LIBRARY
HAROLD WASHINGTON LIBRARY CENTER

R0020400929

LB 2844.1 .A8 N3 — This is your passbook for assistant teacher

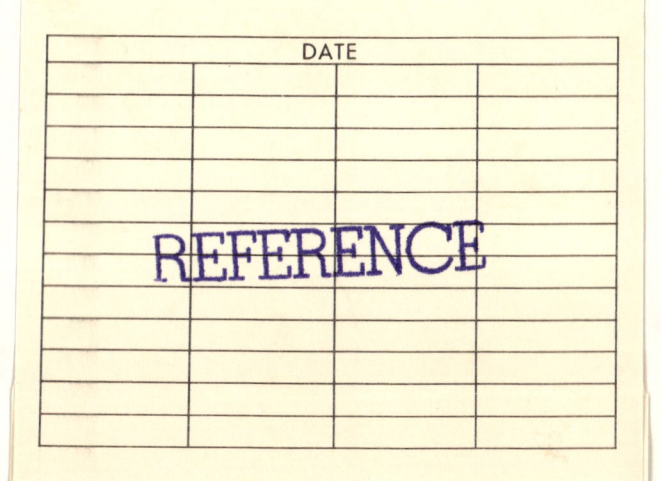

REFERENCE

FORM 125 M

Cop. 1 SOCIAL SCIENCES & HISTORY DIVISION

The Chicago Public Library

Received OCT 2 2 1979

© THE BAKER & TAYLOR CO.

C-1118
ISBN 0-8373-1118-7

THE PASSBOOK® SERIES

PASSBOOKS®

FOR

VOCATIONAL-TECHNICAL CAREERS

ASSISTANT TEACHER

NATIONAL LEARNING CORPORATION

REF
LB
2844.1
.A8
N3

Cop.1

All rights reserved, including the right of reproduction in whole or in part, in any form or by any means, electronic or mechanical, including photocopying, recording, or by any information storage and retrieval system, without permission in writing from the Publisher.

Copyright © 1977 by **National Learning Corporation**
212 Michael Drive, Syosset, New York 11791
(516) 921-8888

PRINTED IN THE UNITED STATES OF AMERICA

PASSBOOK SERIES®

The *PASSBOOK SERIES* has been created to prepare applicants and candidates for the ultimate academic battlefield – the examination room.

At some time in our lives, each and every one of us may be required to take an examination – for validation, matriculation, admission, qualification, registration, certification, or licensure.

Based on the assumption that every applicant or candidate has met the basic formal educational standards, has taken the required number of courses, and read the necessary texts, the *PASSBOOK SERIES* furnishes the one special preparation which may assure passing with confidence, instead of failing with insecurity. Examination questions – together with answers – are furnished as the basic vehicle for study so that the mysteries of the examination and its compounding difficulties may be eliminated or diminished by a sure method.

This book is meant to help you pass your examination provided that you qualify and are serious in your objective.

The entire field is reviewed through the huge store of content information which is succinctly presented through a provocative and challenging approach – the question-and-answer method.

A climate of success is established by furnishing the correct answers at the end of each test.

You soon learn to recognize types of questions, forms of questions, and patterns of questioning. You may even begin to anticipate expected outcomes.

You perceive that many questions are repeated or adapted so that you gain acute insights, which may enable you to score many sure points.

You learn how to confront new questions, or types of questions, and to attack them confidently and work out the correct answers.

You note objectives and emphases, and recognize pitfalls and dangers, so that you may make positive educational adjustments.

Moreover, you are kept fully informed in relation to new concepts, methods, practices, and directions in the field.

You discover that you are actually taking the examination all the time: you are preparing for the examination by "taking" an examination, not by reading extraneous and/or supererogatory textbooks.

In short, this PASSBOOK, used directedly, should be an important factor in helping you to pass your test.

PROFESSIONAL EDUCATION

EXAMINATION SECTION

CONTENTS

	Page
TEST 1	1
TEST 2	3
TEST 3	6
TEST 4	9
TEST 5	12
KEYS (CORRECT ANSWERS)	16

PROFESSIONAL EDUCATION

EXAMINATION SECTION

CONTENTS

	Page
TEST 1	1
TEST 2	4
TEST 3	7
TEST 4	9
TEST 5	13
KEYS (CORRECT ANSWERS)	16

EXAMINATION SECTION

CONTENTS

TEST 1

    KEY (CORRECT ANSWERS)

TEST 2

    KEY (CORRECT ANSWERS)

TEST 3

    KEY (CORRECT ANSWERS)

TEST 4

    KEY (CORRECT ANSWERS)

TEST 5

    KEY (CORRECT ANSWERS)

EXAMINATION SECTION

CONTENTS

TEST 1

KEY (CORRECT ANSWERS)

TEST 2

KEY (CORRECT ANSWERS)

TEST 3

KEY (CORRECT ANSWERS)

TEST 4

KEY (CORRECT ANSWERS)

TEST 5

KEY (CORRECT ANSWERS)

EXAMINATION SECTION

CONTENTS

TEST 1

    KEY (CORRECT ANSWERS)

TEST 2

    KEY (CORRECT ANSWERS)

BASIC PRINCIPLES AND PRACTICES IN EDUCATION
THE NEW PROGRAM OF EDUCATION

CONTENTS

I. PHILOSOPHY AND OBJECTIVES — 1
   A. Philosophy — 1
   B. Concepts of Education — 1
   C. Objectives — 1
   D. Methods of Achieving These Objectives — 2
   E. Organismic Psychology — 2
   F. Underlying Tenets of the Program — 2
   G. What Does the New Program Mean? — 3
   H. Advantages and Disadvantages — 3
   I. Traditional vs. Progressive Education — 4
   J. General Principles in Any Modern Philosophy of Elementary Education — 4

II. THE CURRICULUM — 5
   A. Definitions — 5
   B. General Considerations — 5
   C. Conditions that Compel Curricular Changes — 6
   D. Changes that Result From Curriculum Improvement — 6
   E. Main Problems in Curriculum Development — 6
   F. Factors Affecting Curriculum Programs — 7
   G. Considerations for Curriculum Programs — 7
   H. Questions Related to Curriculum Development — 7

III. GROUPING AND COMMITTEE WORK — 8
   A. Organizing Groups for Instruction — 8
   B. Criteria for Group Work — 8
   C. Committee Work — 9

IV. EVALUATION — 9
   A. Items to be Evaluated — 9
   B. Reasons for Evaluating — 10
   C. Who Evaluates? — 10
   D. Evaluation in a Unit of Work — 10

V. DISCIPLINE — 12
   A. Meaning — 12
   B. Discipline vs. Order — 12
   C. The Difference Between Conduct and Behavior — 12

V. DISCIPLINE (cont'd) — 12
   D. Planes of Discipline — 12
   E. General Principles of Classroom Discipline — 13
   F. Positive vs. Negative Discipline — 13
   G. Why Some Teachers Have Disciplinary Troubles — 13
   H. Class Morale as a Factor in Classroom Discipline — 13
   I. The Use of Incentives — 14
   J. Classroom Punishments — 15
   K. Some Practical Suggestions for Teachers (Characteristic of Transition from Order to Discipline) — 17

VI. BASIC FUNDAMENTALS OF EDUCATIONAL PSYCHOLOGY — 17
   A. Conditioning — 17
   B. Learning by Trial and Error (Connectionism) — 18
   C. Learning by Insight: Gestalt Psychology — 18
   D. The Field Theory (Organismic, Holistic Theory) — 18
   E. Transfer of Training — 19
   F. Habit — 20
   G. Individual Differences — 21

VII. HISTORY OF EDUCATION — 21
   A. Leaders — 21
      1. Socrates — 21
      2. Plato — 22
      3. Aristotle — 22
      4. Comenius — 22
      5. Locke — 22
      6. Rousseau — 22
      7. Basedow — 23
      8. Pestalozzi — 23
      9. Herbart — 23
      10. Froebel — 23
      11. Spencer — 23
      12. Mann — 23
      13. Barnard — 24
      14. Dewey — 24
   B. Conceptualized Definitions and Aims of Education — 24

HOW TO TAKE A TEST

You have studied hard, long, and conscientiously.

With your official admission card in hand, and your heart pounding, you have been admitted to the examination room.

You note that there are several hundred other applicants in the examination room waiting to take the same test.

They all appear to be equally well prepared.

You know that nothing but your best effort will suffice. The "moment of truth" is at hand: you now have to demonstrate objectively, in writing, your knowledge of content and your understanding of subject matter.

You are fighting the most important battle of your life -- to pass and/or score high on an examination which will determine your career and provide the economic basis for your livelihood.

What extra, special things should you know and should you do in taking the examination?

BEFORE THE TEST

YOUR PHYSICAL CONDITION IS IMPORTANT

If you are not well, you can't do your best work on tests. If you are half asleep, you can't do your best either. Here are some tips:
1. Get about the same amount of sleep you usually get. Don't stay up all night before the test, either partying or worrying -- DON'T DO IT.
2. If you wear glasses, be sure to wear them when you go to take the test. This goes for hearing aids, too.
3. If you have any physical problems that may keep you from doing your best, be sure to tell the person giving the test. If you are sick or in poor health, you really cannot do your best on any test. You can always come back and take the test some other time.

AT THE TEST

EXAMINATION TECHNIQUES

1. Read the *general* instructions carefully. These are usually printed on the first page of the examination booklet. As a rule, these instructions refer to the timing of the examination; the fact that you should not start work until the signal and must stop work at a signal, etc. If there are any *special* instructions, such as a choice of questions to be answered, make sure that you note this instruction carefully.

2. When you are ready to start work on the examination, that is as soon as the signal has been given, read the instructions to each question booklet, underline any key words or phrases, such as *least, best, outline, describe,* and the like. In this way you will tend to answer as requested rather than discover on reviewing your paper that you *listed without describing,* that you selected the *worst* choice rather than the *best* choice, etc.

3. If the examination is of the objective or so-called multiple-choice type, that is, each question will also give a series of possible answers: A,B,C, or D, and you are called upon to select the best answer and write the letter next to that answer on your answer paper, it is advisable to start answering each question in turn. There may be anywhere from 50 to 100 such questions in the three or four hours allotted and you can see how much time would be taken if you read through all the questions before beginning to answer any. Furthermore, if you come across a question or a group of questions which you know would be difficult to answer, it would undoubtedly affect your handling of all the other questions.

4. If the examination is of the essay-type and contains but a few questions, it is a moot point as to whether you should read all the questions before starting to answer any one. Of course if you are given a choice, say five out of seven and the like, then it is essential to read all the questions so you can eliminate the two which are most difficult. If, however, you are asked to answer all the questions, there may be danger in trying to answer the easiest one first because you may find that you will spend too much time on it. The best technique is to answer the first question, then proceed to the second, etc.

5. Time your answers. Before the examination begins, write down the time it started, then add the time allowed for the examination and write down the time it must be completed, then divide the time available somewhat as follows:
   a. If 3 1/2 hours are allowed, that would be 210 minutes. If you have 80 objective-type questions, that would be an average of about 2 1/2 minutes per question. Allow yourself no more than 2 minutes per question, or a total of 160 minutes, which will permit about 50 minutes to review.
   b. If for the time allotment of 210 minutes, there are 7 essay questions to answer, that would average about 30 minutes a question. Give yourself only 25 minutes per question so that you have about 35 minutes to review.

6. The most important instruction is *to read each question* and make sure you know what is wanted. The second most important instruction is to *time yourself properly* so that you answer every question. The third most important instruction is to *answer every question*. Guess if you have to but include something for each question. Remember that you will receive no credit for a blank and will probably receive some credit if you write something in answer to an essay question. If you guess a letter, say "B" for a multiple-choice question, you may have guessed right. If you leave a blank as the answer to a multiple-choice question, the examiners may respect your feelings but it will not add a point to your score.
7. Suggestions
   a. Objective-Type Questions
      (1) Examine the question booklet for proper sequence of pages and questions.
      (2) Read all instructions carefully.
      (3) Skip any question which seems too difficult; return to it after all other questions have been answered.
      (4) Apportion your time properly; do not spend too much time on any single question or group of questions.
      (5) Note and underline key words -- *all, most, fewest, least, best, worst, same, opposite*.
      (6) Pay particular attention to negatives.
      (7) Note unusual option, e.g., unduly long, short, complex, different or similar in content to the body of the question.
      (8) Observe the use of "hedging" words - *probably, may, most likely, etc.*
      (9) Make sure that your answer is put next to the same number as the question.
      10) Do not second guess unless you have good reason to believe the second answer is definitely more correct.
      (11) Cross out original answer if you decide another answer is more accurate; do not erase.
      (12) Answer all questions; guess unless instructed otherwise.
      (13) Leave time for review.

   b. Essay-Type Questions
      (1) Read each question carefully.
      (2) Determine exactly what is wanted. Underline key words or phrases.
      (3) Decide on outline or paragraph answer.
      (4) Include many different points and elements unless asked to develop any one or two points or elements.
      (5) Show impartiality by giving pros and cons unless directed to select one side only.
      (6) Make and write down any assumptions you find necessary to answer the question.
      (7) Watch your English, grammar, punctuation, choice of words.
      (8) Time your answers; don't crowd material.

8. Answering the Essay Question
Most essay questions can be answered by framing the specific response around several key words or ideas. Here are a few such key words or ideas:
   M's: manpower, materials, methods, money, management

   P's: purpose, program, policy, plan, procedure, practice, problems, pitfalls, personnel, public relations

   a. Six basic steps in handling problems:
      (1) preliminary plan and background development
      (2) collect information, data and facts
      (3) analyze and interpret information, data and facts
      (4) analyze and develop solutions as well as make recommendations
      (5) prepare report and sell recommendations
      (6) install recommendations and follow up effectiveness

   b. Pitfalls to Avoid
      (1 *Taking things for granted*
         A statement of the situation does not necessarily imply that each of the elements is necessarily true; for example, a complaint may be invalid and biased so that all that can be taken for granted is that a complaint has been registered.
      (2) *Considering only one side of a situation*
         Wherever possible, indicate several alternatives and then point out the reasons you selected the best one.
      (3) *Failing to indicate follow up*
         Whenever your answer indicates action on your part, make certain that you will take proper follow-up action to see how successful your recommendations, procedures, or actions turn out to be.
      (4) *Taking too long in answering any single question*
         Remember to time your answers properly.

PROFESSIONAL EDUCATION EXAMINATION SECTION

DIRECTIONS FOR THIS SECTION:
Each question or incomplete statement is followed by several suggested answers or completions. Select the one that BEST answers the question or completes the statement. *PRINT THE LETTER OF THE CORRECT ANSWER IN THE SPACE AT THE RIGHT*.

TEST 1

1. Locke's great influence was not exerted *until*
    A. Comenius made his ideas practical
    B. Rousseau set forth is views
    C. Ratke popularized his views in METHODUS NOVA
    D. Bacon issued his ADVANCEMENT OF LEARNING

2. In the NOVUM ORGANUM, there was formulated
    A. the catechetical method
    B. the method of inductive reasoning
    C. the reorganization of the sciences
    D. a system of encyclopaedic education

3. The theory of formal discipline was championed CHIEFLY by the
    A. Humanists   B. Sophists   C. Realists   D. Behaviorists

4. In the ORGANON, Aristotle formulated a(n)
    A. code of moral conduct
    B. method of scientific politics
    C. method of deductive reasoning
    D. ideal system of State education

5. The teaching of history and literature was emphasized by Herbart chiefly for their
    A. patriotic value   B. practical value
    C. social value   D. content value

6. Horace Mann is BEST known for
    A. bringing Pestalozzian methods to America
    B. establishing free, nonsectarian education
    C. establishing high schools
    D. establishing State boards of education

7. The "Indus" was the elementary school of the
    A. Athenians   B. Romans
    C. early Christians   D. monks of the Middle Ages

8. The RATIO STUDIORUM encouraged
    A. pupil participation in the recitations
    B. initiative of the teachers
    C. differentiation of subject matter to meet the needs of the pupils
    D. free discipline

9. The OUTSTANDING characteristic of the content of Chinese education was its emphasis upon
    A. human relationships   B. material prosperity
    C. property rights   D. intellectual progress

10. The type of education during the Renaissance movement known as "Ciceronianism" stressed
    A. breadth of learning   B. social reform
    C. grace of style   D. intellectual freedom

11. "Negative education," according to Rousseau, meant
    A. compelling a pupil arbitrarily to learn something
    B. using artificial incentive to stimulate the pupil to study

1

C. permitting the pupil to learn what he feels the need of knowing
D. instructing the child in the duties that belong to a man

12. Which one of the following ideas may NOT be ascribed to Comenius?   12. ...
    A. A graded system of schools for both boys and girls beginning in infancy and continuing through the university
    B. An improved method of teaching languages
    C. The use of objective methods
    D. A complete separation in aims and objectives of the church and the school

13. Which of the following statements is NOT true? Froebel   13. ...
    A. accepted Rousseau's emphasis upon the rights of childhood
    B. agreed with Pestalozzi that education is the harmonious development of all the powers of the individual
    C. has greatly influenced our present educational system
    D. accepted Rousseau's belief that the child should have little or no social training

14. The educational tendency with which the name of John Locke is associated is   14. ...
    A. humanistic   B. disciplinary
    C. naturalistic   D. psychological

15. A name *largely* identified with investigation in the field of reading is   15. ...
    A. Ayres   B. Stanford   C. Yerkes   D. Gray

16. Colonial America was MOST interested in   16. ...
    A. primary education   B. advanced education
    C. agricultural education   D. commercial education

17. The Puritans in New England, in respect to elementary education, believed in   17. ...
    A. compulsory maintenance   B. pauper school maintenance
    C. church maintenance   D. voluntary maintenance

18. The FIRST city public school system to introduce kindergartens was   18. ...
    A. Boston   B. Oswego   C. St. Louis   D. Philadelphia

19. The name of the learning theory associated with Skinner is the   19. ...
    A. Reinforcement Theory
    B. Trial and Error Learning Theory
    C. Sign Learning Theory   D. Conditioned Response Theory

20. Of the following concepts, the one LEAST consonant with John Dewey's philosophy of education is   20. ...
    A. learning through experience   B. extrinsic motivation
    C. emphasis on the learner rather than on the subject
    D. democracy and pragmatism

21. Dr. James Bryant Conant wrote all of the following EXCEPT   21. ...
    A. THE SCHOOLS   B. SLUMS AND SUBURBS
    C. MODERN SCIENCE AND MODERN MAN
    D. EDUCATION IN A DIVIDED WORLD

22. Which one of the following educators is NOT noted for his work in the field of intelligence testing?   22. ...
    A. Louis Terman   B. Rudolph Pintner
    C. David Wechsler   D. Robert Hutchins

23. Spearman is known for his concept of intelligence as consisting of
    A. the interaction of numerous specific and general factors
    B. a single general factor
    C. a general factor and many specific factors
    D. a limited number of specific factors
24. The concept of the IQ was introduced by
    A. Binet   B. Goddard   C. Stern   D. Witmer
25. Which one of the following statements is TRUE with regard to the "activity program?"
    A. The child is displaced as the center of the educative process.
    B. Maximum preparation for effective group living is considered essential.
    C. The learning of a definite body of factual material is stressed.
    D. Distinct effort is made to keep children "up to standard" in drill subjects.

TEST 2

1. In planning a trip to a market in connection with a core on food,
    A. the teacher should ask all the children to observe carefully and to report on as many different things as they see
    B. a committee composed of a few children should be held responsible for formulating a report on the trip
    C. definite questions should be formulated before the trip is taken for the purpose of finding answers to them
    D. questions need not be provided, since follow-up activities should be left to the initiative of the pupils
2. In order to secure good group play activities in her class, the teacher of a class should plan
    A. classroom procedures with a view to minimizing individual play activities on the part of her children
    B. for personal participation in every group play activity which is organized
    C. to play with small groups several times before the children play without her
    D. to set aside one day a week for independent group play activity
3. The instrument MOST useful for determining interpersonal relationships in the classroom is the
    A. Vineland Social Maturity Scale
    B. Kuder Preference Record
    C. sociogram   D. California Test of Personality
4. The IQ of a pupil is determined by the following formula:
    A. MA/CA   B. CA/MA   C. CA/SM   D. MA/SM
5. John and Paul have mental ages of 9-4 on the Stanford-Binet, Form L. From these results, it can be inferred that *each*
    A. will achieve at about the same level
    B. has an equivalent vocabulary

C. may be quite different in intellectual functioning
D. has the same level of aspiration

6. Mary and Helen each have an IQ of 67 on the Stanford-Binet, Form M. Mary has a reading grade of 3.4 and Helen a reading grade of 3.2. These data *suggest* that
    A. the reading level is in terms of the IQ for both
    B. Mary's IQ must be higher because her reading grade is higher
    C. Helen's progress in general will be slower
    D. general school achievement cannot be predicted from the above results

7. Basal age on the Stanford-Binet means
    A. one year below the actual mental age
    B. the year level up through which all the test items are passed
    C. one year above the actual chronological age
    D. the lowest year level at which all the test times are failed

8. A notation on a psychologist's report reads as follows: "Lucy is at the 30th percentile on this test when compared with the norms for her age group." This means that Lucy
    A. exceeded 30% of her age group
    B. had answered 30% of the questions correctly
    C. had failed 30% of the questions
    D. was exceeded by 30% of her age group

9. Which *one* of the following names is identified with school achievement testing?
    A. Goodenough   B. Henmon-Nelson
    C. Metropolitan   D. Kuhlmann-Anderson

10. A child in your class scores 2.7 in an arithmetic test. His IQ is 69. Which of the following is the MOST important in determining whether or not he is working at capacity?
    A. Mean and standard deviation for the class
    B. Range of scores for the class
    C. Chronological age   D. Social intelligence

11. Andrew uses a large wheel on his desk to steer an imaginary car. He is frequently heard to say, "Make that light," "Turn this way," "Slow down," etc.
His behavior is an example of
    A. sublimation B. fantasy C. retrogression D. introjection

12. Ronald, a severely retarded boy in your class, tells the other children that he will join the air force and become a famous pilot. He is using the adjustive mechanism of
    A. abreaction   B. conversion
    C. compensation   D. reaction-formation

13. A motor disturbance that lacks any appearance of purpose beyond the action itself is called a(n)
    A. phobia   B. tic   C. compulsion D. obsession

14. The child reacts to the classroom situation in terms of his
    A. intelligence   B. home background
    C. social development   D. past experience

15. Several children have complained that the other children in the school "push them around" in the school cafeteria. You *should*

A. arrange for the children to eat earlier or later than the other children
   B. discipline the children who were accused
   C. indicate that if the pupils were better behaved, they would not be "pushed around"
   D. treat it as a problem usual among all children
16. The day before the Easter Vacation the mother of one of your boys tells you that she plans a trip to Washington, D.C., for the school holiday period and that she hesitates to take the boy with her because he may be too dull to benefit by the trip. You *should suggest*
   A. leaving him with his grandmother
   B. that she board him out for the period involved
   C. an early appointment with the school social worker
   D. that she take the child with her
17. The principal asks the teachers in a junior high school how they feel regarding their classes' participation in the school's safety patrol unit. As the teacher of a class in this school, your reply should be that the children of your class
   A. are likely to be injured in this kind of activity
   B. will not be obeyed by the other children in the school
   C. would not like this kind of assignment
   D. would be glad to participate
18. A widely used sight vocabulary list of 220 words *other than* nouns has been prepared by
   A. Gray   B. Dolch   C. Gates   D. Thorndike
19. The teacher of a class of adolescent students feels the need for a test of oral reading performance in order to obtain a more comprehensive picture of the reading skills of her group. A test MOST suitable for this purpose was devised by
   A. Thorndike   B. Harris   C. Gray   D. Kirk
20. The MOST important reason why basal readers are usually inadequate for the slow learner is the
   A. over-abundance of illustrations
   B. insufficient repetition accorded new words
   C. heavy vocabulary load
   D. discrepancy between pupil interests and content
21. In developing functional reading materials on a third-grade level for one of the reading groups in a class of retarded students, the teacher should
   A. refer to the Thorndike lists for the vocabulary to be used and integrate the material with the core being taught
   B. extract interesting material from basal readers employing a vocabulary they can read with ease
   C. integrate the material with the core being taught employing a functional vocabulary not exceeding the third year level
   D. integrate the material with the core being taught, employing the functional vocabulary necessary even if it exceeds the third year level
22. In teaching spelling, the BEST procedure is
   A. an incidental method best suited to each individual

      B. the application of a minimum number of basic rules
         for spelling
      C. to permit the student to use his own methods
      D. a systematic method with the entire group
23. The spelling words to be taught to children should be
      A. those functional words which are most often mispelled
         in children's writings
      B. Board of Education spelling lists for the grade levels
         involved
      C. those functional words which center about the core
      D. those words which they will write in their everyday
         living
24. A teacher must recognize that specific skills
      A. must be taught apart from other learnings in order
         to be most effective
      B. can rarely be integrated with the curricular core
      C. are to be tied into the core experience
      D. are to be taught on occasion as the situation calls
         for them
25. John, a withdrawn child, often brings curious objects to
    class, such as dead frogs, a broken clock, and pictures
    from old magazines. The teacher *should*
      A. ignore his bizarre behavior as much as possible
      B. speak to him privately about leaving such objects at
         home
      C. hold the objects for him until the end of the day
      D. organize class discussions around the objects

TEST 3

1. Of the following techniques, the one that is of MOST value
   to the junior high school teacher in curricular planning is
      A. sociograms   B. projective tests
      C. problem checklists D. anecdotal records
2. In order to use standardized test results as a basis for a
   remedial program for a class, a teacher *should*
      A. use the average grade score made by the class to deter-
         mine the level at which to begin instruction
      B. begin instruction at the level attained by the poorest
         pupil
      C. use the items failed by pupils making the highest
         scores to determine the topics which need emphasis
      D. analyze the items most frequently failed to develop
         an inventory of common errors
3. In general, the MOST powerful predictors of subsequent
   vocational successes have been
      A. personality tests   B. interest tests
      C. clinical interviews D. school records
4. The distinction between aptitude tests and achievement
   tests is CHIEFLY one of
      A. type of content   B. predictive power
      C. purpose for which used D. breadth of content
5. The FUNDAMENTAL characteristic which Binet and Simon believed their early intelligence tests tapped was the
      A. ability to make sound judgments

    B. speed of reaction to oral stimuli
    C. understanding of oral directions
    D. ability to develop vocabulary

6. Of the following terms, the *one* that applies to the development of wholesome mental and emotional reactions and habits is called
    A. psychoanalysis   B. psychotherapy
    C. mental hygiene   D. clinical psychology

7. The term *ambivalent* is used to describe a child who
    A. is given to creating dissension among the others
    B. makes a statement and later amplifies it with conscious intent
    C. seems to be day dreaming while actually alert
    D. is aggressive at times and friendly at other times

8. The symbol "AQ" is used to denote the *result* of
    A. $\frac{IQ}{MA}$ B. $\frac{MA}{EA}$ C. $\frac{EA}{AA}$ D. $\frac{AA}{MA}$

9. The term *commonly* used in statistics to refer to the average of a group of scores is the
    A. mean   B. mode   C. central tendency   D. median

10. The BASIC function of the educational and vocational counselor in a coordinated junior high school guidance program is
    A. maintaining adequate guidance records
    B. assembling and disseminating vocational information
    C. work with individual children
    D. coordinating the resources of community agencies

11. When an instrument used as a counseling tool measures what it *purports* to measure, it
    A. has validity   B. has reliability
    C. is standardized   D. is objective

12. A *case study* is a
    A. rating of a pupil's development used in guiding his educational and vocational choices and in correcting personality faults
    B. developmental record of facts and insights about an individual
    C. story of the pupil's life written by the pupil himself
    D. narrative of events in which the pupil reveals something which may be significant about his personality

13. The formula, $\frac{EA}{MA}$,
    A. gives an index showing whether a personal knowledge and understanding of a group of school subjects are commensurate with his life age
    B. yields a quotient which shows whether or not the individual is working up to capacity
    C. yields a ratio of one's mental age to one's life age
    D. indicates each pupil's position in the hierarchy of intelligence

14. Sociometric testing provides a technique for
    A. analyzing each person's position and status within the group with respect to a particular criterion
    B. revealing the prejudices of each individual
    C. obtaining a picture of boy-girl relationships
    D. analyzing the pupil's understanding of the problems faced by society and encouraging efforts to solve them

15. In the field of psychological testing, the term *norm* may   15. ...
be used to designate
    A. the relationship between the score of the individual
       and the average of the group
    B. a central tendency of the scores of a specific group
    C. the stages in the intellectucal development of
       individuals
    D. the relationship between intellectual maturity and
       the psychological maturity of the group
16. To be of value, anecdotal records of a pupil *should*   16. ...
    A. describe the teacher's reactions as well as the be-
       havior of the child
    B. objectively describe the child's behavior
    C. be shown to the pupil regularly so that he can see
       himself as others see him
    D. be periodically circulated among the pupil's teachers
       so that they may have a better knowledge of what to
       expect of this pupil
17. A psychological report indicates that a student has been   17. ...
given a Rorschach test. This was used to
    A. test mental ability   B. discover interests
    C. determine artistic talent
    D. evaluate personality adjustment
18. Three personality inventories or rating scales suitable   18. ...
for use with junior high school pupils are:
    A. Bell Adjustment Inventory, Bernreuter Personality
       Inventory, Allport A-S Reaction Study
    B. Minnesota Personality Scale, California Test of
       Mental Maturity, Allport-Vernon Study of Values
    C. California Test of Personality, Haggerty-Olson-Wick-
       man Behavior Rating Schedules, Washburne Social Ad-
       justment Inventory
    D. Minnesota Multiphasic Personality Inventory, Hurm-
       Wadsworth Temperament Scale, Dearborn Group Tests
19. THE SCIENCE OF THE EARTH IN RELATION TO NATURE AND THE   19. ...
HISTORY OF MAN was written by
    A. Humboldt   B. Guyot   C. Ritter   D. Froebel
20. Concerning "formal discipline," Spencer held that   20. ...
    A. it was untenable   B. only the classics could effect it
    C. scientific studies could effect it
    D. scientific studies could not effect it
21. The methods used in the schools of Lancaster and Bell were   21. ...
    A. mechanical, inelastic and without psychological founda-
       tion
    B. unorganized, wasteful and unproductive
    C. individual, expensive and grossly inefficient
    D. suited as far as possible to the individual needs of
       the pupils
22. "I wish to psychologize education" is a well-known state-   22. ...
ment by
    A. Herbart   B. Froebel   C. James   D. Pestalozzi
23. The Public School Society was associated with   23. ...
    A. New York   B. Philadelphia   C. Boston   D. Charleston
24. First in order of time, in the history of American educa-   24. ...
tion, came the

A. high school
B. Latin grammar school
C. academy
D. normal school

25. The *chief* argument for unification of the first grade and kindergarten is found MAINLY in the fact that
    A. there is no historical justification for the separation
    B. correlation may be secured
    C. there is a large overlapping of mental ages in the two grades
    D. additional drill in the tool subjects may be given to all

TEST 4

1. *Good* teacher-pupil planning in a class entails
    A. acceptance of all pupil suggestions
    B. strict adherence to the plan
    C. the teacher's playing a minor role in the planning session
    D. teacher and class evaluation of their success in achieving the plan

2. The MOST important reason why the teacher of a class should group for instruction is to
    A. make her job easier
    B. meet individual needs and differences realistically
    C. give the children a feeling of working together
    D. avoid conducting the class solely on an individual basis

3. Of the following objectives, the *one* of LEAST importance in the teaching of art in the elementary grades is to
    A. provide an outlet of expression for children
    B. produce finished, artistic pieces of work
    C. promote artistic growth in children
    D. increase sensitivity to fine art forms

4. Of the following charges against the modern school, the MOST valid is that it has
    A. to a large degree neglected the teaching of the basic skills
    B. to a large degree emphasized and condoned "loose" or "free" discipline
    C. to a large degree ignored moral and spiritual values
    D. resulted in interpreting "continuous progress" to mean "100% promotion"

5. Of the following, the BEST reason for emphasis on science in the elementary school is to enable the elementary school curriculum to
    A. play its proper role in a program of improvement of education
    B. be based on the need for America to live in a "climate of science"
    C. play the major role in coping with the problems of the gifted child
    D. answer the scientific advances made through the Russian schools

TEST 4

6. Given only the information that most "juvenile delinquents" 6. ...
come from low socio-economic neighborhoods, the conclusion
that such neighborhoods cause the delinquency is *logically*
based on all of the following assumptions EXCEPT
   A. no other more basic factors cause both the juvenile
      delinquency and the poor neighborhoods
   B. the higher incidence of such delinquency in low socio-
      economic areas is not due to chance
   C. juvenile delinquency is more serious when it occurs
      in poor neighborhoods
   D. the same definition of delinquent behavior has been
      applied to all socio-economic levels of juveniles

7. To have all children in a given grade in a certain city   7. ...
reading at or above "grade norm" for that grade in that
city is
   A. *desirable* since the "norm" represents a minimum for
      the grade
   B. *immaterial* since the "norm" is merely an arbitrary
      number set up by "experts" in reading
   C. *difficult* because the "norm" represents a maximum goal
      intended as a motivating device
   D. *impossible* without changing the "norm" because the
      "norm" represents the average for the grade

8. Of the following choices for the basis of the goals of   8. ...
education, the one which is BEST is
   A. the needs of the child
   B. the goals of our democratic society
   C. a combination of A and B
   D. the expressed values and wishes of the parents

9. Of the following, the one which is the LEAST valuable   9. ...
reason for considering art an essential area of school
experience for elementary school children is that it
   A. provides all children with a means of self-realization
   B. affords excellent opportunities for children to become
      aware of the values of orderliness, planning and care
      of materials
   C. provides a way of utilizing, developing and integrating
      the whole child, nor merely his mental and verbal capac-
      ities
   D. allows the gifted child to find himself

10. Of the following purported characteristics of slow learn- 10. ...
ers, the one which is *usually* TRUE is that they are
   A. as much interested in gaining recognition and success
      in school as faster learners are
   B. very good in manual work
   C. usually motivated by tasks that require constant
      repetition and little understanding
   D. usually superior to their chronological peers in
      physical development

11. Of the following possible first steps for helping an awk- 11. ...
ward child overcome his fear of playground activities,
the one which is *usually* BEST is to
   A. give him some easy task connected with the game -
      "keeping score," for example
   B. send him to another classroom during the game period

C. insist that he get into the game and play immediately
D. allow him to work or do something else, alone

12. The last name of the present Secretary of the Department 12. ...
of Health, Welfare and Education is (1975)
A. Hobby B. Folsom C. Blossom D. None of these

13. Of the following statements about unusually bright or 13. ...
gifted young children, the one which is INCORRECT is that
they are
A. generally superior in size, muscular control and
general health to others of the same age
B. usually one-sided in their emotional development
C. usually not eccentric, not queer, and no more unstable
than children of "average" mental ability
D. often difficult to identify at an early age

14. Of the following choices, the one which is MOST effective 14. ...
for a teacher to use in trying to learn as much as possi-
ble about her children is
A. standardized tests
B. informal methods, such as folders of actual work or
conferences with the child and his parents
C. observation of the child's behavior and performance
D. a combination of all of the above

15. Of the following, the one which is LEAST useful as a 15. ...
practical guide for drill is
A. it is better to have a little practice on many skills
than much practice on a few skills
B. a drill exercise should be specific
C. understanding must precede drill
D. it is good to have a scoring technique for drill which
allows a pupil to watch his daily and weekly progress

16. A VERY important part of "good discipline" in elementary 16. ...
schools involves
A. teaching children what is acceptable as well as what
is not acceptable behavior in specific circumstances
B. allowing the children to make nearly all of their own
decisions
C. expecting the children to act like "little ladies and
gentlemen" most of the time
D. adjusting pupil behavior to suit the occasion by allowing complete permissiveness when there are no visitors
and requiring absolute quiet when adult company comes

17. In connection with the study of the International Geo- 17. ...
physical Year, the one of the following TV programs BEST
for elementary school children was
A. Mr. Wizard   B. Science Fiction Theatre
C. "See It Now"   D. "80,000 Leagues Under the Sea"

18. An unusually worthwhile TV program called "Sunrise Semes- 18. ...
ter" which featured the study of great classics in literature was conducted by
A. Clifton Fadiman   B. Bergen Evans
C. Hal March   D. Floyd Zulli, Jr.

19. Teaching of all subjects in the elementary school should 19. ...
be
A. on an individual basis
B. varied to meet the needs of individuals, of groups,
and of the whole class

C. geared to the normal youngsters who make up the majority of the class
D. always by the unit approach
20. The school should begin the study of science when the 20. ...
   A. child enters the fifth grade   B. child enters school
   C. average child enters the junior high school
   D. child has begun to study geography
21. In discussing discipline at an individual parent-teacher 21. ...
meeting, the teacher should try to get the parent to understand the meaning of discipline as
   A. immediate punishment for an infraction of a rule
   B. complete permissiveness so as not to develop any sense of frustration or failure
   C. self-control developed over a long period through understanding, kindness, firmness, and consistency
   D. immediate and unquestioning obedience at all times to adults in authority
22. The IQ is PRIMARILY a measure of 22. ...
   A. scholastic aptitude   B. interest in verbal activities
   C. achievements in the 3 R's
   D. ability to adjust to school
23. Of the following statements regarding juvenile delin- 23. ...
quency, the one that is *most nearly* true is they
   A. almost invariably come from families of low economic level
   B. are almost invariably of a low intellectual level
   C. are usually more mature socially and physically than other children
   D. often suffer from a combination of emotional illness and lack of conscience
24. The term which *most clearly* expresses the psychological 24. ...
basis of modern educational practice is
   A. atomistic   B. organismic
   C. analytic   D. behavioristic
25. In developing good character traits in young children, 25. ...
the BEST of the following techniques is *probably*
   A. short dramatic discussions on good behavior
   B. TV programs which have good behavior as "the moral"
   C. administration of a personality test and follow-up discussion of the results
   D. the desired type of behavior on the part of the adults with whom the children come into contact regularly

TEST 5

DIRECTIONS: In each of the following questions there is a pair of numbered sentences. Each pair is followed by four lettered choices. Select the choice which indicates your judgment concerning the accuracy of the information contained in *each* of the pairs. PRINT THE LETTER OF THE CORRECT ANSWER IN THE SPACE AT THE RIGHT.

1. I. WINDOWS FROM THE CROWN PRINCE is a book dealing with 1. ...
the experiences of a teacher in the Far East.
   II. Two plays dealing with the experiences of teachers are "The King and I" and "Bells are Ringing."

TEST 5

    A. Both I and II are correct
    B. Both I and II are incorrect
    C. I is correct; II is incorrect
    D. I is incorrect; II is correct

2. I. Jean Jacques Rousseau based his philosophy of education on his theory of man's natural perfection or perfectibility.
  II. William James was an exponent of pragmatism.
    A. Both I and II are correct
    B. Both I and II are incorrect
    C. I is correct; II is incorrect
    D. I is incorrect; II is correct

2. ...

3. I. The Constitution of the United States clearly provides for equal educational opportunities for all.
  II. The administrative emphasis in the American public school system is upon decentralization and local control.
    A. Both I and II are correct
    B. Both I and II are incorrect
    C. I is correct; II is incorrect
    D. I is incorrect; II is correct

3. ...

4. I. Deprivation of privileges as a means of discipline is most effective if it is logically related to the child's misbehavior.
  II. Deprivation of privileges as a means of discipline is most effective if it is not delayed but immediately follows the misbehavior.
    A. Both I and II are correct
    B. Both I and II are incorrect
    C. I is correct; II is incorrect
    D. I is incorrect; II is correct

4. ...

5. I. The resource unit is designed to provide a guide for the teacher, prescribing exact content and procedures.
  II. Resource units are likely to be most effective when they are used by the group that had no hand in their preparation.
    A. Both I and II are correct
    B. Both I and II are incorrect
    C. I is correct; II is incorrect
    D. I is incorrect; II is correct

5. ...

6. I. To discover how much her children are benefiting from classroom instruction, a teacher should use the Stanford-Binet Scale or the Wechsler Intelligence Scale.
  II. Standardized tests are of significant value in the guidance of children.
    A. Both I and II are correct
    B. Both I and II are incorrect
    C. I is correct; II is incorrect
    D. I is incorrect; II is correct

6. ...

7. I. In parent-teacher conferences, it is easier to build a cooperative relationship if the teacher is not seated behind her desk.
  II. In parent-teacher conferences, the teacher should bear in mind the fact that most parents cannot be objective about their own children.
    A. Both I and II are correct
    B. Both I and II are incorrect

7. ...

        C. I is correct; II is incorrect
        D. I is incorrect; II is correct
 8.   I. Kindergarten children who do not skip should be   8. ...
          taught to do so.
      II. Children should not be permitted to read in the
          kindergarten.
        A. Both I and II are correct
        B. Both I and II are incorrect
        C. I is correct; II is incorrect
        D. I is incorrect; II is correct
 9.   I. Kindergarten training in the U.S.S.R. is on a very   9. ...
          formal basis and does not include most of the activi-
          ties carried on in the American kindergarten.
      II. A primary objective in the kindergarten is to increase
          children's facility in the use of oral language.
        A. Both I and II are correct
        B. Both I and II are incorrect
        C. I is correct; II is incorrect
        D. I is incorrect; II is correct
10.   I. Parents of kindergarten children should never be per-   10. ...
          mitted to stay in the classroom with their children.
      II. Kindergarten children who cry on entering school and
          refuse to leave their parents should be referred to a
          psychologist.
        A. Both I and II are correct
        B. Both I and II are incorrect
        C. I is correct; II is incorrect
        D. I is incorrect; II is correct
11.   I. In the elementary school, guidance and teaching are   11. ...
          inseparable.
      II. Guidance is concerned primarily with causes, rather
          than with symptoms.
        A. Both I and II are correct
        B. Both I and II are incorrect
        C. I is correct; II is incorrect
        D. I is incorrect; II is correct
12.   I. Science experiments have no place in the kindergarten. 12. ...
      II. "Just listening" to music has a place in the kinder-
          garten.
        A. Both I and II are correct
        B. Both I and II are incorrect
        C. I is correct; II is incorrect
        D. I is incorrect; II is correct
13.   I. The "Corsi Bill" permitting corporal punishment in   13. ...
          schools was passed by the New York State Legislature
          and was vetoed by the Governor.
      II. Homogeneous grouping on the basis of IQ assures classes
          of similar abilities in reading and mathematics.
        A. Both I and II are correct
        B. Both I and II are incorrect
        C. I is correct; II is incorrect
        D. I is incorrect; II is correct
14.   I. There is a high correlation between success in read-   14. ...
          ing and achievement in other fields.
      II. There is a high correlation between success in mathe-
          matics and IQ.

A. Both I and II are correct
B. Both I and II are incorrect
C. I is correct; II is incorrect
D. I is incorrect; II is correct

15. I. Following the Supreme Court decision banning segregated schools, all states have undertaken at least token integration of the races in their schools.
    II. Congress recently passed a bill making direct grants to the various states for the purpose of increasing teachers' salaries.
    A. Both I and II are correct
    B. Both I and II are incorrect
    C. I is correct; II is incorrect
    D. I is incorrect; I is correct

16. I. The five-year-old cannot work for prolonged periods of time, and is not capable of completing a project.
    II. Differences are great even among "typical" children.
    A. Both I and II are correct
    B. Both I and II are incorrect
    C. I is correct; II is incorrect
    D. I is incorrect; II is correct

17. I. Lack of language facility is a significant factor in the negativism and resistance to authority which are normal for five-year-olds.
    II. At times a kindergarten teacher is justified in arbitrarily assigning children to groups or tasks without regard for their preferences.
    A. Both I and II are correct
    B. Both I and II are incorrect
    C. I is correct; II is incorrect
    D. I is incorrect; II is correct

18. I. UNESCO, an agency of the United Nations, has as its principal objective, the promotion of a world government.
    II. The National Education Association is an agency of the Federal Government.
    A. Both I and II are correct
    B. Both I and II are incorrect
    C. I is correct; II is incorrect
    D. I is incorrect; II is correct

19. I. A. T. Jersild is a writer in the field of child psychology.
    II. James L. Hymes has written extensively on the teaching of reading.
    A. Both I and II are correct
    B. Both I and II are incorrect
    C. I is correct; II is incorrect
    D. I is incorrect; II is correct

20. I. Comenius based his philosophy of education on his theory of man's perfection or perfectibility.
    II. Maria Montessori emphasized the necessity of play in the education of the young child.
    A. Both I and II are correct
    B. Both I and II are incorrect
    C. I is correct; II is incorrect
    D. I is incorrect; II is correct

KEYS (CORRECT ANSWERS)

TEST 1	TEST 2	TEST 3	TEST 4	TEST 5
1. B	1. C	1. C	1. D	1. C
2. B	2. B	2. D	2. B	2. A
3. C	3. C	3. D	3. B	3. D
4. C	4. A	4. C	4. D	4. A
5. C	5. C	5. A	5. A	5. B
6. A	6. D	6. C	6. C	6. D
7. B	7. B	7. D	7. D	7. A
8. B	8. A	8. D	8. C	8. C
9. A	9. C	9. A	9. D	9. D
10. C	10. C	10. C	10. A	10. B
11. C	11. B	11. A	11. A	11. C
12. D	12. C	12. B	12. D	12. D
13. D	13. B	13. B	13. B	13. C
14. B	14. D	14. A	14. D	14. A
15. D	15. D	15. B	15. A	15. B
16. A	16. D	16. B	16. A	16. D
17. B	17. D	17. D	17. A	17. A
18. C	18. B	18. C	18. D	18. B
19. A	19. B	19. C	19. B	19. C
20. B	20. D	20. C	20. B	20. B
21. A	21. D	21. A	21. C	
22. D	22. D	22. D	22. A	
23. C	23. D	23. A	23. D	
24. C	24. C	24. B	24. B	
25. B	25. D	25. C	25. D	

PROFESSIONAL EDUCATION
EXAMINATION SECTION

DIRECTIONS FOR THIS SECTION:
Each question or incomplete statement is followed by several suggested answers or completions. Select the one that BEST answers the question or completes the statement. *PRINT THE LETTER OF THE CORRECT ANSWER IN THE SPACE AT THE RIGHT*.

TEST 1

1. The objective of *all* art experiences in the elementary grades is to
    A. develop the ability to draw realistically
    B. keep children busy with motor activity
    C. secure a uniform standard and type of expression
    D. promote emotional stability, uscular coordination, and originality of expression

2. An attractive and orderly classroom
    A. exerts a silent influence on children and helps them to improve their sense of order and taste
    B. is unnoticed by children but good when parents visit the school
    C. can be enhanced with crepe paper curtains and color transparencies on windows or doors
    D. is possible in new buildings but completely out of the question in old buildings

3. The arts are included in the program of the elementary school CHIEFLY because they
    A. provide an opportunity to discover artistic talent
    B. provide rest and relaxation from studies which involve mental activity
    C. provide emotional release, motor coordination, and another means of communication
    D. make it possible to illustrate and add color and interest to units of study

4. Children will become sensitive to color variations and better able to use color for personal expression *if* they
    A. learn to identify primary and secondary colors and if they make color wheels using those colors
    B. have many opportunities to choose, use and judge colors in many materials and for many uses
    C. make many designs using analogous and complementary color harmonics
    D. copy color-reproductions of paintings by the old masters

5. Art and craft activities should be emphasized for low IQ pupils because
    A. art activities do not require ability to think or to judge
    B. they can be furnished with patterns to follow
    C. art gives them another and practical way of learning from doing
    D. they will have articles and gifts to take home

6. When a fourth-grade boy says, "I want to draw my street, but I can't make it look right," the teacher should aid him by
    A. giving him a book of perspective to study and copy

1. ...
2. ...
3. ...
4. ...
5. ...
6. ...

TEST 1

  B. having him observe carefully similar forms from the classroom window, the corridor or his own street
  C. having him learn the rules of perspective and then make diagrams of blocks above and below eye level in parallel and angular perspective
  D. suggesting that he draw something else which does not involve perspective

7. Of the following, the approach *usually* MOST effective in developing an efficient, happy classroom is
  A. promptly and appropriately punishing every infraction of class rules
  B. developing the habit of automatic obedience in the children
  C. keeping parents constantly informed of their children's level of behavior
  D. planning interesting and appropriate activities to meet the needs of the individual children

8. Among the contributions made by the "Gestalt" psychologists is the idea that
  A. the individual reacts to a total environment
  B. a particular isolated stimulus will lead to a specific response
  C. the best method of learning is through "conditioning"
  D. each "faculty" of the brain must be provided with appropriate exercise

9. The development of the contemporary curricular program in elementary education is PRIMARILY associated with the ideas of
  A. Henry Barnard   B. John Dewey
  C. Horace Mann   D. Edward Thorndike

10. Public schools in the United States receive from the Federal Government
  A. the major part of their financial support, amounting to more than 75% of the total
  B. half of their financial support, the Government matching combined state and local amounts
  C. a small proportion of their total financial support
  D. no financial support

11. The term *correlation* differs from the term *integration* in that the former
  A. is narrower in meaning   B. is broader in meaning
  C. has no relationship to integration
  D. is opposite in meaning to integration

12. In current educational philosophy and practice, guidance is considered to be
  A. the province of the trained practitioner exclusively
  B. a matter of relatively minor importance
  C. the concern of all teachers
  D. a matter for agencies other than the school

13. The PRINCIPAL use of a diagnostic test is to
  A. measure achievement
  B. determine weaknesses as a basis for remedial instruction
  C. discover aptitudes
  D. evaluate previous teaching procedures

14. The MOST important purpose for using achievement tests is to measure

    A. capacity for future learning
    B. quality and quantity of previous learning
    C. vocational or educational aptitude
    D. quality and quantity of previous teaching

15. Of the following, the phrase which has been MOST widely used to describe contemporary developments in American secondary education is:
    A. Activity program
    B. Education for life adjustment
    C. Return to fundamentals
    D. Education for defense of democracy

16. The one of the following which is NOT a book-list for secondary schools is
    A. Reader's Digest of Books
    B. Reading Ladders for Human Relations
    C. Books for You   D. Your Reading

17. The one of the following which is a device to be used in group dynamics is a(n)
    A. metronoscope   B. opaque projector
    C. diorama   D. sociogram

18. The one of the following persons who is NOT a leader in the field of English education is
    A. Angela M. Broening   B. Channing Pollack
    C. Lou La Brant   D. Robert C. Pooley

19. A teacher, in assigning an essay to be read, tells the class that there will be a special test on this assignment and that the mark on the test will count for a large proportion of the next report-card grade.
This is considered *poor* motivation CHIEFLY because it
    A. is likely to discourage poor readers
    B. gives the better readers an unfair advantage
    C. is not easily understood by pupils
    D. is extrinsic and places undue emphasis on marks

20. In planning a lesson in which a film is to be shown to the class, it is *advisable*
    A. not to tell the class anything about it in advance in order that interest may be high
    B. to tell the class to pay close attention to what they are going to see because a quiz will follow the showing
    C. to assume that the film need not be related to the work of the class as long as they enjoy seeing it
    D. to conduct a preparatory discussion and a follow-up in which the relationship of the film to the work of the class is established

21. Teaching grammar *functionally* means
    A. teaching only what you are sure pupils will need and use in later life
    B. teaching the functions of parts of speech and parts of the sentence
    C. using diagrams, charts, and stick figures
    D. emphasizing usage skills and the relationship between grammar and meaning

22. In a distribution of test scores, the BEST measure, among the following, of central tendency is the

      A. average deviation   B. mode
      C. median   D. standard-deviation
23. All of the following publications are intended particularly for teachers EXCEPT
      A. THE ENGLISH JOURNAL   B. ELEMENTARY ENGLISH
      C. HIGH POINTS   D. PRACTICAL ENGLISH
24. When grading pupil compositions, the BEST method of correction is to
      A. underline the error and indicate the nature of it in the margin by using a correction symbol
      B. assign a general comment to encourage the pupil
      C. correct the errors he has made by writing in the proper form yourself
      D. underline the error without indicating the nature of it
25. As a means of cultivating literary appreciation, oral reading is
      A. superior to silent reading   B. the only method to use
      C. inferior to silent reading
      D. ineffective because it is slower than silent reading

TEST 2

1. The norms accompanying a standardized test should be looked upon as scores that
      A. pupils of a given age or grade should make
      B. the teacher should set as a goal for her class
      C. have been made by a large group of pupils of a given age or grade
      D. the pupils should set as a goal for themselves
2. Of the following types of tests, the one that would *probably* yield the HIGHEST correlation with scholastic achievement is
      A. memory span   B. sentence completion
      C. weight discrimination   D. arithmetic computation
3. A technique that is NOT used to detect color blindness is
      A. Ishihara   B. Snellen   C. Holmgren   D. Farnsworth
4. Of the following expressions, the one which CANNOT *by itself* be used to interpret an individual score on an intelligence test is
      A. standard deviation   B. standard score
      C. percentile   D. deviation I. Q.
5. The *original* selection of items for an intelligence test would depend PRIMARILY upon the
      A. discriminative ability of the items
      B. interest value to the group for which the scale was intended
      C. simplicity of the response, which would facilitate scoring
      D. concept of intelligence held by the test constructor
6. Of the following intelligence tests, the one which is NOT a *group* test is the
      A. Pintner-Cunningham   B. Pintner-Paterson
      C. Pintner-Durost   D. Kuhlmann-Anderson

7. A survey test is *generally* used to
   A. yield a precise measure of individuals
   B. measure group status
   C. locate specific areas of weakness or strength
   D. yield a measure of an individual's ability to learn in some particular area

8. A technique using the drawing of a man as a measure of intelligence was developed by
   A. Raven   B. Pintner   C. Goodenough   D. R. B. Cattell

9. In deciding upon the inclusion of a specific item in a pupil personnel record, the MOST important consideration is whether the item
   A. represents objective data
   B. has value to the pupil as used by school staff members
   C. has reliability when reported by a number of school staff members
   D. may be readily interpreted by guidance staff members dealing with the pupil

10. The MOST valid reason for keeping pupil personnel records is to
    A. form a basis for referral to community agencies and for reports to higher institutions
    B. provide a basis for distribution of pupils among classes of a grade
    C. provide data for educational research on the basis of which educational improvements are planned
    D. improve instruction and guidance for the pupil

11. An ailment which does NOT occur as a functional disorder is
    A. tuberculosis   B. stomach cramps
    C. hysterical paralysis D. stammering

12. The mental mechanism of minimizing one's own faults and deficiencies by criticizing and blaming others is known as
    A. compensation   B. rationalization
    C. transference   D. projection

13. Sibling rivalry is the term used to describe the competitive feeling between two or more individuals *who*
    A. are in the same school grade
    B. are children of the same parents
    C. have similar goals of achievement
    D. are in the same chronological age group

14. Of the following, the *single* characteristic MOST important in determining an individual's status in a group of pre-adolescent boys is
    A. intelligence   B. physical ability
    C. school marks   D. language development

15. Research has shown that neighborhood gangs tend to be more cohesive than groups of the same age functioning as clubs in more formal youth agencies. This would suggest that
    A. the club is potentially longer-lived than the gang
    B. young people join clubs only if they are not accepted by the gang
    C. clubs will not be able to function adequately in a given neighborhood until some way is found to destroy gangs already in existence

D. the activities of the gang meet the needs of its members better than those of the club program do
16. The individual who emerges as the leader of a group is *usually*
   A. the person who, in the judgment of the group, can best meet the demands of the particular problem
   B. superior to the other members of the group in a wide variety of abilities
   C. chosen on the basis of personal qualities rather than ability
   D. the same person, no matter in what activities the group participates
17. The status of an individual in a group is determined, *for the most part*, by
   A. the possession of those qualities the group deems important
   B. his socio-economic level
   C. his status in other groups of which he is a member
   D. the amount of time and energy he is willing to devote to the purposes of the group
18. Experiments using arithmetic as the subject under consideration have shown that pupils make more progress when they work for themselves than when they work for the progress of the group. This finding *probably* means that
   A. group work does not provide an adequate incentive for maximum achievement
   B. pupils are generally self-centered and selfish
   C. the subject of arithmetic was not important enough to the pupils
   D. the pupils did not consider the group of significance to them
19. Of the following, the BEST way to deal with a 12-year-old boy who feels inferior to his peers is to
   A. provide tasks which he can master with little difficulty
   B. show him how irrational his feelings are
   C. accept his declarations of lack of confidence sympathetically
   D. carefully arrange situations in which he will be obliged to show leadership
20. The professional educator should know that Social Security or Old Age and Survivors Insurance is paid for by
   A. taxes deducted from the employee's salary only
   B. funds set aside by the federal government from income taxes
   C. the state in which the worker lives at the time of his retirement or death
   D. taxes deducted from the employee's salary plus an equal amount paid by the employer
21. Studies involving the relative mental abilities of delinquent and non-delinquent children have *generally*
   A. shown that there are no significant differences between them
   B. shown that delinquent children are slightly but significantly brighter than non-delinquents
   C. shown that non-delinquent children are somewhat brighter than delinquent children

D. been about evenly divided- some finding the delinquent children brighter, others finding mental superiority for non-delinquents
22. Current evidence and thinking on the causative factors in juvenile delinquency support the view that
    A. social factors are more basic than psychological factors
    B. psychological factors are more basic than social factors
    C. psychological factors and social factors are of about equal importance
    D. physiological factors are more important than either social or psychological factors
23. Of the following, the behavior which would be considered MOST indicative of potential or actual maladjustment in a junior high school boy is
    A. treating his classmates to sodas in an attempt to buy their votes in a school election
    B. spending his entire allowance each week on science fiction paperbacks
    C. finding fault with the work of his classmates
    D. failing to take care of school property
24. Of the following teachers, the one MOST liked by the largest number of junior high school pupils is the one who
    A. sets easily attainable standards
    B. demonstrates a high level of intellectual competence
    C. maintains an impersonal objective attitude
    D. is sympathetic
25. Of the following characteristics, the one MOST generally found among children just entering the junior high school is
    A. a tendency of boys and girls to seek each other's company
    B. the acceptance of parent and teacher opinion with little question
    C. the popularity of guessing games, puzzles, and games of chance
    D. a preference for highly organized competitive team play

TEST 3

1. Starch's study of school ratings showed that the correlation in ratings received in any elementary subject with other elementary subjects was
   A. high   B. low but positive   C. negligible   D. negative
2. According to Thorndike, negative correlations between different efficiencies are
   A. rare   B. common
   C. found only in bright pupils   D. found only in adults
3. In the formation of habitual reactions, there is a transference of regulative function from the brain to subcortical levels
   A. finally   B. sometimes   C. usually   D. never

TEST 3

4. The plateau phenomenon, often found in human learning, does   4. ...
NOT exist in animal learning experiments because
    A. animals are unable to spurt in learning
    B. animals are unable to profit by errors
    C. the incentive in animal learning is constant
    D. animals have weak incentives in learning
5. The typical learning curve rises rapidly *at first* usually   5. ...
because the
    A. learner is enthusiastic
    B. measurement of initial response is exaggerated
    C. beginning is always made easy
    D. abscissa is arranged to that end
6. All learning is bond connecting; this principle does NOT   6. ...
apply to
    A. habits   B. reflexes   C. skills   D. attitudes
7. On the basis of mental age, MOST bright children in the   7. ...
average school are, as concerns grading,
    A. accelerated B. retarded   C. normal   D. much accelerated
8. Studies show that children who make exceptionally good   8. ...
records in elementary grades
    A. also make superior records in high school
    B. do only normal work in high school
    C. do poor work in high school
    D. do superior work in only one or two high school subjects
9. Terman's studies of superior children show that in moral   9. ...
and personal traits
    A. they are below normal
    B. they are evenly distributed about the norm
    C. the superiority is especially marked
    D. the superiority is marked except in social adaptability
10. Terman's studies of superior children indicate that their   10. ...
school work is such in most cases as to warrant promotion
to a grade closely corresponding to the mental age in
    A. a few cases   B. most cases
    C. no case   D. all cases
11. "Transfer of training" occurs MORE fully *among*   11. ...
    A. morons   B. dull individuals
    C. bright individuals   D. normal individuals
12. The penalty imposed on an offending pupil by the class   12. ...
teacher should be
    A. administered immediately
    B. primarily retributive and based solely upon the damage done
    C. punitive   D. adjusted to the motive behind the offense
13. Problems of class management and of discipline should be   13. ...
considered in the light of the principle that the
    A. interests of the school and of the individual pupil are identical
    B. school is nothing; the child is all
    C. interests of any individual must always give way before those of the group of which he is a member
    D. interests of the school are supreme and must be maintained
14. Probably the MOST potent cause of nervous breakdown is   14. ...

    A. mental fatigue   B. physical fatigue
    C. ennui   D. emotional stress
15. The MOST effective preventive and remedy for fear is   15. ...
    A. coordinated motor activity of any kind
    B. inhibition of mental activity
    C. transfer of training   D. sudden change of stimuli
16. Delusions of grandeur or persecution are *typical* of   16. ...
    A. paranoia B. hysteria C. dementia praecox D. chorea
17. Plasticity or modifiability of the nervous system is   17. ...
    GREATEST
    A. at birth   B. between the ages of 6 and 12
    C. between the ages of 13 and 18   D. in adult life
18. The sympathetic division of the autonomic nervous system   18. ...
    is connected with the
    A. lower part of the spinal cord
    B. upper part of the cord and the midbrain
    C. intermediate part of the cord   D. upper part
19. In psychology, the term *reaction* refers to   19. ...
    A. all kinds of responses that the organism makes to
       stimuli
    B. muscular responses   C. cortical changes only
    D. reflexes and instincts
20. A synpase is   20. ...
    A. a tree-like cell body with its nucleus and branches
    B. a glia cell
    C. any place where the nerve impulse from one neuron
       may be passed on to another neuron
    D. the sending end of a neuron
21. In all trial and error reaction, improvement is NOT apt   21. ...
    to come *if* the response is
    A. annoying to the individual
    B. entirely satisfactory to the individual
    C. repeated once   D. repeated often
22. Education must *always* start with   22. ...
    A. habits   B. attitudes
    C. instinctive tendencies   D. inhibitions
23. "Reciprocal modification" is a technical term in psychol-   23. ...
    ogy that refers to
    A. forgetting   B. transfer of training
    C. conditioned reflex   D. physiological limit
24. It has been fairly well demonstrated that the ability to   24. ...
    speak or write words depends upon connections established
    in the
    A. reflex level route   B. cortical level
    C. midbrain and adjoining part of central nervous system
    D. sensory neurons
25. The motor area of a man's brain was destroyed in an ac-   25. ...
    cident. It is NOT true that because of this he *cannot*
    A. walk   B. run his typewriter
    C. use a knife and fork D. sing a song

TEST 4

1. Standardized group tests are used MORE frequently than   1. ...
   individual tests, because

A. the same amount of time is needed to test a whole class by a group approach as a single pupil by an individual approach
B. group tests give better results than individual tests
C. group tests have primary, intermediate and advanced forms whereas individual tests have only one form
D. no training is needed to administer a group test

2. Of the following statements about marks, the one which is NOT correct is:
   A. Excessive emphasis on marks may cause the pupil to consider the mark more important than the material to be learned.
   B. The pupil may rely too heavily on mere memory in order to get high marks.
   C. Occasionally, overemphasis on marks may lead to cheating.
   D. Marks based solely on written tests give a valid measure of a pupil's achievement because they are always objective.

3. Standardized achievement tests are characterized by *all* of the following principles EXCEPT they
   A. often show differing results, depending upon the particular form of the test used
   B. are administered in accordance with uniform procedures indicated in the manual of instructions
   C. have norms for grade or age
   D. are scored in accordance with standard procedures indicated in the manual of instructions

4. Of the following, the PRIME purpose of grouping pupils in a mathematics class is to
   A. develop social attitudes   B. separate unruly pupils
   C. provide the teacher with a smaller range of pupil ability or disability
   D. help solve book shortages

5. Of these statements concerning grouping, select the one which is CONTRARY to present-day thinking:
   A. In a math class, grouping enables the teacher to meet individual differences.
   B. Results of inventory tests may be used as one of the bases for forming groups.
   C. Teachers should avoid attaching any status value to groups.
   D. Once in a group, a pupil should be kept there for the rest of the year.

6. Of the following statements about slow pupils, the one which is *most nearly* CORRECT is that they
   A. are always unruly
   B. should be given plenty of busy work
   C. usually have a short attention span
   D. should seldom be given homework

7. Of these statements concerning the use of the overhead projector, which one is NOT true? It
   A. may not be used with a page of the textbook
   B. enables the teacher to observe the class reaction
   C. may be used with transparencies and with overlays
   D. requires an additional person to operate it

TEST 4

8. Of these statements concerning the use of audio-visual aids, which one is NOT true?
   A. Students are helped to learn faster.
   B. They help students to gain more accurate information.
   C. They help students to perceive and understand meanings.
   D. They substitute for, rather than supplement, instructional techniques.

9. Homework should be assigned regularly in the junior high school, because, among other values,
   A. doing homework aids in the development of more independent study habits
   B. survey results indicate that pupil progress is proportional to the amount of homework assigned
   C. homework keeps pupils out of mischief at home
   D. it is traditional to assign homework, and parents demand it

10. In planning a homework assignment, the teacher should observe which one of the following principles? The assignment should
    A. review material previously taught as well as material taught on the day that the assignment was given
    B. be limited to material taught on the day that the assignment was given
    C. not include any material taught on the day the assignment was given
    D. be done only by those pupils who have not fallen so far behind that they cannot profit from doing the assignment

11. The BEST homework assignment to assist junior high school pupils to prepare for a test is which one of the following? To
    A. tell them to study for a test
    B. give them a set of problems identical to those that will appear on the test
    C. tell them to prepare a set of questions they think should appear on the test
    D. tell them the scope of the test and to assign specific study references and specific practice material covering the scope

12. Which one of the following statements is CONTRARY to present thinking?
    A. Most teachers regard homework as important.
    B. Experimental evidence is not clearly convincing that homework is truly important.
    C. The voluntary type of assignment in which the pupil does whatever he thinks is necessary is the solution to the homework dilemma.
    D. Many parents think homework is helpful.

13. Which of the following is the BEST approach to the use of the text book by a teacher of mathematics?
    A. Only as a source of practice exercises
    B. Primarily as a source of problems to be placed on tests
    C. To assist pupils in learning how to read explanations of new concepts and techniques
    D. Primarily for review

14. Of the following, the LEAST proper use of the textbook is as 14. ...
    A. a quick view of things to be learned
    B. a minimum for which pupils may be held responsible
    C. the course of study
    D. a reference for pictures, maps, graphs, tables
15. Of the following statements concerning questioning, which one is NOT consistent with current thinking? 15. ...
    A. Some questions, though perfect in form, may challenge only a limited number of pupils.
    B. Vague and incomplete questions tend to confuse pupils.
    C. "Chorus" answers do not afford all pupils an opportunity to think.
    D. Questions starting with "why" and "how" should generally be avoided.
16. Of the following, the problems which are of LEAST value in stimulating real thinking are those 16. ...
    A. which pupils solve in many ways
    B. which pupils solve in one way which has been thoroughly practiced
    C. in which pupils encounter extraneous data
    D. which pupils cannot solve because of insufficient data
17. Of the following, select the suggestion LEAST likely to help a pupil having difficulty in finding the solutions to a verbal problem. 17. ...
    A. Generalize the problem by using letters instead of numbers
    B. Estimate the answer   C. Use round numbers
    D. Use diagrams or representations
18. In order to implement the aims and objectives of the junior high school, the mathematics teacher should NOT 18. ...
    A. make certain to study each child as an individual and provide for the normal, bright, and slow learners
    B. encourage and help pupils to explore and sample the fields of algebra, geometry, and trigonometry
    C. assist all pupils in acquiring competence in independent study through effective study habits
    D. encourage all pupils to go on to college
19. Of the following, the one that LEAST describes a principle of classroom motivation is that 19. ...
    A. the motivation should be brief
    B. the motivation should be related to the new work being introduced
    C. the motivation should be related to the experiences of the pupils
    D. interest in the subject for its own sake is always an adequate motivation
20. The CORRECT order of teaching-learning pattern, which involves the following processes: 20. ...
    I. Application of problems   II. Computations
    III. Experiences   IV. Thinking though
    is in the sequence:
    A. I, II, III, IV   B. III, IV, II, I
    C. II, III, IV, I   D. IV, I, II, III
21. Select the one of the following principles of learning mathematics which is NOT correct: 21. ...

12

A. Pupils learn as individuals even though they are taught in groups.
B. It should be expected that all pupils can master all elements of mathematics at the same grade and age.
C. Individual instruction in mathematics is occasionally or even often necessary.
D. Each pupil tends to learn only in terms of his active interest and participation.

22. When teaching a new topic, the teacher should   22. ...
    A. make sure that all homework difficulties have been corrected before teaching the new material
    B. allow sufficient time for a full presentation of the new material
    C. teach the new material before any discussion of the homework
    D. warn pupils that they will be tested on the new material the next day

23. In a comparison of the developmental and lecture methods   23. ...
    of teaching, which one of the following statements is *most nearly* CORRECT?
    A. In the lecture method, the teacher readily checks the progress of learning.
    B. There is greater pupil participation in the developmental method.
    C. Greater pupil attention is insured in the lecture method.
    D. There is less need for review at the beginning of a developmental lesson.

24. A benefit resulting from the introduction of numbers in   24. ...
    other bases than 10 into the curriculum of junior high school mathematics is that
    A. this results in better understanding of the number system in base 10
    B. there is a better basis for problem solving
    C. computation is simpler with numbers in bases other than 10
    D. fewer digits are required for numbers in bases other than 10

25. Of the following, the statement concerning deductive   25. ...
    proofs which is CORRECT is that they
    A. have no place in the junior high school mathematics curriculum
    B. help junior high school pupils to understand and to appreciate the sequential nature of mathematics
    C. can be used only in geometry
    D. should not be used before a pupil reaches the 9th grade

TEST 5

DIRECTIONS: In each of the following questions there is a pair of numbered sentences. Each pair is followed by four lettered choices. Select the choice which indicates your judgment concerning the accuracy of the information contained in each of the pairs.

TEST 5

1. I. One important aspect of good mental health is freedom from anxiety and tension.
   II. Intelligence test ratings are not an indication of the person's full potential for solving life's problems.
      A. Both I and II are correct
      B. Both I and II are incorrect
      C. I is correct; II is incorrect
      D. I is incorrect; II is correct

1. ...

2. I. A valid and reliable group test, if well administered, may still result in some individual scores which are misleading.
   II. Gestalt psychology maintains that context plays an important part in determining what we perceive.
      A. Both I and II are correct
      B. Both I and II are incorrect
      C. I is correct; II is incorrect
      D. I is incorrect; II is correct

2. ...

3. I. A longitudinal study is one in which the same children are measured or evaluated over a period of years.
   II. THE JOURNAL OF THE NEA and SEVENTEEN are both periodicals dealing with educational matters for the most part.
      A. Both I and II are correct
      B. Both I and II are incorrect
      C. I is correct; II is incorrect
      D. I is incorrect; II is correct

3. ...

4. I. Children should never leave their seats without the permission of the teacher.
   II. It is often advisable for the teacher to repeat a correct answer so that the entire class will hear it clearly.
      A. Both I and II are correct
      B. Both I and II are incorrect
      C. I is correct; II is incorrect
      D. I is incorrect; II is correct

4. ...

5. I. Children's experiences outside of the school become part of the curriculum if they are used by the school to further the aims of its program.
   II. If the teacher plans carefully and effectively at home, the necessity for pupil-teacher planning in the classroom is considerably lessened.
      A. Both I and II are correct
      B. Both I and II are incorrect
      C. I is correct; II is incorrect
      D. I is incorrect; II is correct

5. ...

6. I. It is wise for a teacher to let no act of misbehavior go unpunished.
   II. A teacher can help reduce juvenile delinquency by holding all her pupils to rigid standards of achievement.
      A. Both I and II are correct
      B. Both I and II are incorrect
      C. I is correct; II is incorrect
      D. I is incorrect; II is correct

6. ...

7. I. There are times when a teacher should deal with behavior itself rather than with the causes of that behavior.
   II. A normal child is made to feel more secure by the knowledge that there are limits to what he is permitted

7. ...

14

to do, and that his parents and teachers will consistently hold to these limits.
   A. Both I and II are correct
   B. Both I and II are incorrect
   C. I is correct; II is incorrect
   D. I is incorrect; II is correct
8. I. Prejudices and antagonistic attitudes toward groups other than one's own are the results of learning experiences.
   II. It is wise to deliberately expose a child to frustrations early in life, to enable him to learn by experience how to cope with frustrations.
   A. Both I and II are correct
   B. Both I and II are incorrect
   C. I is correct; II is incorrect
   D. I is incorrect; II is correct
9. I. A teacher tends to lose standing in the eyes of pupils if she admits not knowing an answer to a question asked by them.
   II. A friendly, personal relationship between pupil and teacher is essential for some important learning outcomes.
   A. Both I and II are correct
   B. Both I and II are incorrect
   C. I is correct; II is incorrect
   D. I is incorrect; II is correct
10. I. A teacher who genuinely loves her pupils and who shows this love to them will, therefore, rarely have discipline problems.
   II. A teacher can develop good relationships with the children in her class if she leads the children to look upon her as their "pal."
   A. Both I and II are correct
   B. Both I and II are incorrect
   C. I is correct; II is incorrect
   D. I is incorrect; II is correct
11. I. The current major function of evaluation by a teacher is to determine which children should repeat a grade, which should be normally promoted, and which accelerated.
   II. Evaluation by children should be encouraged but limited to their own work and to the work of their classmates.
   A. Both I and II are correct
   B. Both I and II are incorrect
   C. I is correct; II is incorrect
   D. I is incorrect; II is correct
12. I. The setting up of classroom routines should be initiated by a teacher on the first day of the term even though she does not yet know her children.
   II. A school system may actually contribute to social-class differences in the community by virtue of the fact that it often groups together children of similar social status.
   A. Both I and II are correct
   B. Both I and II are incorrect
   C. I is correct; II is incorrect
   D. I is incorrect; II is correct

13. I. Some skills taught in elementary school mathematics are so difficult that it is best to teach them by rote drill, avoiding the time-consuming attempt to rationalize them.
    II. Highly organized athletic competitions, such as interscholastic tournaments and little league games, are appropriate sports activities for children of elementary school age.
    A. Both I and II are correct
    B. Both I and II are incorrect
    C. I is correct; II is incorrect
    D. I is incorrect; II is correct

13. ...

14. I. Children should be permitted to experiment with various art media without step-by-step direction by adults.
    II. Having the children in a class take turns at being committee chairmen in connection with social studies units is very useful in promoting democratic living.
    A. Both I and II are correct
    B. Both I and II are incorrect
    C. I is correct; II is incorrect
    D. I is incorrect; II is correct

14. ...

15. I. If the parents of a maladjusted child refuse to cooperate with the teacher, there is relatively little the teacher can do to help the child adjust.
    II. A knowledge of the goals and objectives of the public school system, as a whole, are of little use to a teacher in that system, concerned with planning her daily teaching activities.
    A. Both I and II are correct
    B. Both I and II are incorrect
    C. I is correct; II is incorrect
    D. I is incorrect; II is correct

15. ...

KEYS (CORRECT ANSWERS)

TEST 1		TEST 2		TEST 3		TEST 4		TEST
1. D	11. A	1. C	11. A	1. A	11. C	1. A	11. D	1.
2. A	12. C	2. B	12. D	2. A	12. D	2. D	12. C	2.
3. C	13. B	3. B	13. B	3. A	13. C	3. A	13. C	3.
4. B	14. B	4. A	14. B	4. A	14. D	4. C	14. C	4.
5. C	15. B	5. D	15. D	5. A	15. D	5. D	15. D	5.
6. B	16. A	6. B	16. A	6. B	16. A	6. C	16. B	6.
7. D	17. D	7. B	17. A	7. B	17. A	7. D	17. A	7.
8. A	18. B	8. C	18. D	8. A	18. C	8. D	18. D	8.
9. B	19. D	9. B	19. A	9. C	19. A	9. A	19. D	9.
10. C	20. D	10. D	20. D	10. B	20. C	10. A	20. B	10.
	21. D		21. C		21. B		21. B	11.
	22. C		22. B		22. C		22. B	12.
	23. D		23. C		23. B		23. B	13.
	24. D		24. D		24. B		24. A	14.
	25. A		25. C		25. D		25. B	15.

EXAMINATION SECTION

TEST 1

DIRECTIONS: Each question or incomplete statement is followed by several suggested answers or completions. Select the one that BEST answers the question or completes the statement. *PRINT THE LETTER OF THE CORRECT ANSWER* THE SPACE AT THE RIGHT.

1. *All* of the following are aspects of the readiness program before systematic instruction in reading is begun, EXCEPT the
    A. keeping of a bulletin board in the classroom with weather reports, special events, or messages to the children
    B. labeling of objects in the classroom such as desks, chairs, and blackboard
    C. use of a pre-primer as an introduction to a reading series
    D. composing of little stories by the children which are recorded on a chart by the teacher

2. *Which one* of the following statements is INCORRECT in regard to the handling of reading difficulties of children?
    A. Poor readers who need training in word recognition should be discouraged from using context clues.
    B. Most authorities agree that auditory discrimination is a factor to be considered in a child's reading performance.
    C. Some authorities advocate the use of mirrors in overcoming reversal errors.
    D. Having the child trace and write words is a technique which is employed by some remedial reading teachers.

3. Where there are animal pets in a classroom their health and safety should be the *responsibility* of the
    A. children who brought the pets
    B. teacher
    C. entire class, working individually or in groups
    D. school custodian

4. In the modern program of teaching mathematics, drill
    A. is unnecessary
    B. is more important than it ever was
    C. should come after understanding has been acquired
    D. is not necessary below grade 3

5. *Which one* of the following statements is true about oral reading? It
    A. has virtually no place in today's classroom
    B. requires an audience situation
    C. should be used mainly with social studies
    D. may be used, but requires no instruction

6. Of the following, the GREATEST problem which presents itself when children do research in 5th- or 6th grade social studies is the
   A. tendency to copy verbatim from reference materials
   B. gathering of research material
   C. tendency of adults to do the work for the child
   D. inability of the child to present his findings to the class

6.___

7. During a parent-teacher conference the teacher should do *all* of the following EXCEPT
   A. put the parent at ease
   B. chastise the parent for things he has been doing
   C. listen to what the parent has to say
   D. invite the parent to express her feeling about the child's activity or development in school

7.___

8. *All* of the following are averages *commonly* used in treating educational data EXCEPT the
   A. mean   B. mode   C. median   D. frequency

8.___

9. *All* of the following statements concerning social relationships in the early school years are usually true EXCEPT:
   A. Groups are small and shift rapidly.
   B. Friends are selected because of propinquity and the accident of sharing objects.
   C. Children play and work with others to satisfy personal rather than social desires.
   D. Friends are selected on the basis of belonging to the same sex.

9.___

10. Of the following statistical expressions, *all* are measures of central tendency EXCEPT
    A. 50th percentile   B. arithmetic mean
    C. mode   D. sigma

10.___

11. A percentile score of 45 is
    A. the score equal to the arithmetic mean of the scores
    B. below the accepted norm
    C. equalled or exceeded by 55% of the scores in the distribution
    D. the same as a score of 45 out of 100

11.___

12. Saying that a child has achieved a reading score "below grade norm" *always* means that his score is below
    A. average for the grade
    B. the acceptable minimum for the grade
    C. that to be expected for his mental age
    D. that to be expected for his chronological age

12.___

13. In general, children's ability to solve problems in reasoning is *most closely* related to *which one* of the following?
    A. School experience   B. Chronological age
    C. Mental age   D. I.Q.

13.___

2. (#1).

6. Of the following, the GREATEST problem which presents itself when children do research in 5th- or 6th- grade social studies is the
   A. tendency to copy verbatim from reference materials
   B. gathering of research material
   C. tendency of adults to do the work for the child
   D. inability of the child to present his findings to the class

7. During a parent-teacher conference the teacher should do all of the following EXCEPT
   A. put the parent at ease
   B. chastise the parent for things he has been doing
   C. listen to what the parent has to say
   D. invite the parent to express her feeling about the child's activity or development in school

8. All of the following are averages commonly used in treating educational data EXCEPT the
   A. mean   B. mode   C. median   D. frequency

9. All of the following statements concerning social relationships in the early school years are usually true EXCEPT:
   A. Groups are small and shift rapidly.
   B. Friends are selected because of propinquity and the accident of sharing objects.
   C. Children play and work with others to satisfy personal rather than social desires.
   D. Friends are selected on the basis of belonging to the same sex.

10. Of the following statistical expressions, all are measures of central tendency EXCEPT
    A. 50th percentile   B. arithmetic mean
    C. mode   D. sigma

11. A percentile score of 45 is
    A. the score equal to the arithmetic mean of the scores
    B. below the accepted norm
    C. equalled or exceeded by 55% of the scores in the distribution
    D. the same as a score of 45 out of 100

12. Saying that a child has achieved a reading score "below grade norm" always means that his score is below
    A. average for the grade
    B. the acceptable minimum for the grade
    C. that to be expected for his mental age
    D. that to be expected for his phrenological age

13. In general, children's ability to solve problems in reasoning is most closely related to which one of the following?
    A. School experience   B. Chronological age
    C. Mental age   D. I.Q.

14. Of the following, *which one* should occur LEAST in a pupil's cumulative record?
    A. Grades and test data
    B. Life history and anecdotal data
    C. Data on physical growth and development
    D. Interpretation and opinion

15. John, who had worked diligently on a mathematics problem which he has had difficulty solving, suddenly "saw" how to solve the problem. This illustrates BEST *which one* of the following?
    A. Retroactive inhibition   B. Insight
    C. Transfer   D. Facilitation

16. In general, mental development *ceases* at
    A. approximately age 20 for boys and 18 for girls
    B. adulthood
    C. physiological maturity
    D. death

17. Sex differences in interests are influenced MAINLY by *which one* of the following?
    A. Heredity   B. Instincts
    C. Physiological factors   D. Cultural experience

18. Generally speaking, the FIRST source, *chronologically*, of racial biases is
    A. the peer group   B. teachers
    C. parents   D. siblings

19. The MOST important of the following elements of a plan for an educational program is
    A. definition of the goals   B. assignment of resources
    C. setting up the time schedule
    D. provision for evaluation

20. It is imperative for a school system to force periodic reconsideration of its specific objectives.

    The MOST important of the following reasons for this dictum is that some objectives may
    A. have lost their usefulness   B. have been overlooked
    C. not be easily attainable
    D. no longer be accepted by the teaching staff

21. Management techniques and processes in school systems, as in other organizations, have a high obsolescence rate and their contributions to rational administration tend to decline.

    The MOST important of the following possible causes for this declination is that
    A. practitioners tend to acquire vested interests
    B. new techniques and processes are developed
    C. techniques and processes cannot sustain an administrative structure
    D. new people require new techniques and procedures

14. Of the following, which one should occur LEAST in a pupil's cumulative record?
    A. Grades and test data
    B. Life history and anecdotal data
    C. Data on physical growth and development
    D. Interpretation and opinion

15. John, who had worked diligently on a mathematics problem which he has had difficulty solving, suddenly "saw" how to solve the problem. This illustrates BEST which one of the following?
    A. Retroactive inhibition   B. Insight
    C. Transfer   D. Facilitation

16. In general, mental development ceases at
    A. approximately age 20 for boys and 18 for girls
    B. adulthood
    C. physiological maturity
    D. death

17. Sex differences in interests are influenced MAINLY by which one of the following?
    A. Heredity   B. Instincts
    C. Physiological factors D. Cultural experience

18. Generally speaking, the FIRST source, chronologically, of racial biases is
    A. the peer group   B. teachers
    C. parents   D. siblings

19. The MOST important of the following elements of a plan for an educational program is
    A. definition of the goals   B. assignment of resources
    C. setting up the time schedule
    D. provision for evaluation

20. It is imperative for a school system to force periodic reconsideration of its specific objectives.

    The MOST important of the following reasons for this dictum is v : some objectives may
    A. have lost their usefulness   B. have been overlooked
    C. not be easily attainable
    D. no longer be accepted by the teaching staff

21. Management techniques and processes in school systems, as in other organizations, have a high obsolescence rate and their contributions to rational administration tend to decline.

    The MOST important of the following possible causes for this declination is that
    A. practitioners tend to acquire vested interests
    B. new techniques and processes are developed
    C. techniques and processes cannot sustain an administrative structure
    D. new people require new techniques and procedures

22. Of the following, the *one* which is *generally* considered by experts in learning theory to be ESSENTIAL to learning is
    A. motivation
    B. at least average intelligence
    C. a competent teacher
    D. ability to read

23. The *MOST* important values of a lesson plan book is to
    A. insure continuity of instruction in the event of the teacher's absence
    B. permit the supervisor to evaluate the quality of work done
    C. enable the teacher to give thought to the work that will be carried on in the class
    D. enable the teacher to dictate important statements

24. *Which one* of the following is the *MOST* justifiable way in which a school may work for social improvement?
    A. Teaching the right side of social and political questions
    B. Encouraging pupils to study and discuss social and political issues
    C. Requiring teachers to give pupils clear reasons why they support a particular social point of view
    D. Teaching pupils not to take sides in social and political issues

25. Studies of the effects of motion pictures on attitudes of children aged nine to twelve show that
    A. the majority of children are markedly upset by exciting pictures
    B. motivation to good conduct is a frequent result of seeing pictures
    C. children accept ideals portrayed in the movies more readily than ideals portrayed in their family experience
    D. films having a definite slant or bias will produce measurable attitudinal changes

---

KEY (CORRECT ANSWERS)

1.	B	11.	C
2.	A	12.	C
3.	B	13.	C
4.	C	14.	B
5.	B	15.	A
6.	B	16.	D
7.	C	17.	D
8.	D	18.	B
9.	A	19.	B
10.	D	20.	B

21. B
22. A
23. B
24. B
25. D

22. Of the following, the one which is generally considered by experts in learning theory to be ESSENTIAL to learning is
    A. motivation
    B. at least average intelligence
    C. a competent teacher
    D. ability to read

23. The MOST important values of a lesson plan book is to
    A. insure continuity of instruction in the event of the teacher's absence
    B. permit the supervisor to evaluate the quality of work done
    C. enable the teacher to give thought to the work that will be carried on in the class
    D. enable the teacher to dictate important statements

24. Which one of the following is the MOST justifiable way in which a school may work for social improvement?
    A. Teaching the right side of social and political questions
    B. Encouraging pupils to study and discuss social and political issues
    C. Requiring teachers to give pupils clear reasons why they support a particular social point of view
    D. Teaching pupils not to take sides in social and political issues

25. Studies of the effects of motion pictures on attitudes of children aged nine to twelve show that
    A. the majority of children are markedly upset by exciting pictures
    B. motivation to good conduct is a frequent result of seeing pictures
    C. children accept ideals portrayed in the movies more readily than ideals portrayed in their family experience
    D. films having a definite slant or bias will produce measurable attitudinal changes

---

KEY (CORRECT ANSWERS)

1. B	11. C
2. D	12. C
3. D	13. C
4. D	14. B
5. B	15. A
6. B	16. D
7. C	17. D
8. D	18. B
9. A	19. B
10. D	20. B

21. B
22. A
23. B
24. B
25. D

TEST 2

DIRECTIONS: Each question or incomplete statement is followed by several suggested answers or completions. Select the one that *BEST* answers the question or completes the statement. *PRINT THE LETTER OF THE CORRECT ANSWER IN THE SPACE AT THE RIGHT.*

1. Of the following characteristics, the one that should be regarded as *MOST* indicative of possible maladjustment in a junior high school girl is
    A. interest in art to the virtual neglect of other subjects
    B. striving for perfect marks in all her school work
    C. getting along easily with all her teachers
    D. lack of interest in boys

   1.___

2. Height and weight curves which have been developed for adolescents show a(n)
    A. *marked spurt* in rate of growth in early adolescence followed by *little change* in later adolescence
    B. *moderately increased rate* in early adolescence followed by a *greatly increased rate* in later adolescence
    C. *steady rate* of growth throughout the adolescent period
    D. *increased rate* of growth in early adolescence followed by a *gradual slowing down*

   2.___

3. Studies of the early history of gifted children reveal that, in general, they begin to walk
    A. and to talk at about the same age as typical children
    B. at an earlier age than typical children but begin to talk at about the same age as typical children
    C. at about the same age as typical children but begin to talk at an earlier age than typical children
    D. and to talk at an earlier age than typical children

   3.___

4. In general, juvenile fiction comprises the major part of the reading choices of
    A. girls between 9 and 13   B. boys of all ages
    C. girls of all ages   D. boys between 12 and 16

   4.___

5. Of the following, a major recreational activity *common* to both 10 and 15-year-old boys and girls is
    A. going to the movies   B. riding a bicycle
    C. watching athletic sports D. social dancing

   5.___

6. Girls tend to be superior to boys at the same age *in*
    A. linguistic fluency   B. speed of reaction time
    C. arithmetical reasoning   D. most forms of perception

   6.___

7. The visual defects of children tend to be overlooked by teachers *because*
    A. visual defects rarely interfere with school work
    B. most visual defects are compensated for by other physical traits
    C. children often learn to make temporary accommodation to their visual defects
    D. visual defects cannot be detected without clinical examination

   7.___

TEST 2

DIRECTIONS: Each question or incomplete statement is followed by several suggested answers or completions. Select the one that BEST answers the question or completes the statement. PRINT THE LETTER OF THE CORRECT ANSWER IN THE SPACE AT THE RIGHT.

1. Of the following characteristics, the one that should be regarded as MOST indicative of possible maladjustment in a junior high school girl is
   A. interest in any to the virtual neglect of other subjects
   B. striving for perfect marks in all her school work
   C. getting along easily with all her teachers
   D. lack of interest in boys

1. _____

2. Height and weight curves which have been developed for adolescents show a(n)
   A. marked spurt in rate of growth in early adolescence followed by little change in later adolescence
   B. moderately decreased rate in early adolescence followed by a greatly increased rate in later adolescence
   C. steady rate of growth throughout the adolescent period
   D. increased rate of growth in early adolescence followed by a gradual slowing down

2. _____

3. Studies of the early history of gifted children reveal that, in general, they begin to walk
   A. and to talk at about the same age as typical children
   B. at an earlier age than typical children but begin to talk at about the same age as typical children
   C. at about the same age as typical children but begin to tal_ at an earlier age than typical children
   D. and to talk at an earlier age than typical children

3. _____

4. In general, juvenile fiction comprises the major part of the reading choices of
   A. girls between 9 and 13   B. boys of all ages
   C. girls of all ages   D. boys between 12 and 16

4. _____

5. Of the following, a major recreational activity common to both 10 and 15-year-old boys and girls is
   A. going to the movies   B. riding a bicycle
   C. watching athletic sports   D. social dancing

5. _____

6. Girls tend to be superior to boys at the same age in
   A. linguistic fluency   B. speed of reaction time
   C. arithmetical reasoning   D. most forms of perception

6. _____

7. The visual defects of children tend to be overlooked by teachers because
   A. visual defects rarely interfere with school work
   B. most visual defects are compensated for by other physical traits
   C. children often learn to make temporary accommodation to their visual defects
   D. visual defects cannot be detected without clinical examination

7. _____

8. Research has demonstrated that there is an increase in racial prejudice during adolescence. Of the following, the factor that contributes MOST significantly to this increase is
   A. dislike for deviants from norms of social groups
   B. influence of parental opinion
   C. segregation of groups in school and community
   D. fear of economic pressure from minority groups

   8.___

9. When we compare young children and adolescents with respect to the relative effectiveness of distributed and concentrated practice as a learning technique we find that
   A. young children learn better by distributed practice; adolescents, by concentrated practice
   B. young children learn better by concentrated practice; adolescents, by distributed practice
   C. both young children and adolescents learn better by concentrated practice
   D. both young children and adolescents learn better by distributed practice

   9.___

10. A child develops a headache every time a particularly distasteful task is announced. This type of reaction is characterized as
    A. hysterical   B. rationalization
    C. projection   D. physiological

    10.___

11. The principle of the conditioned response as formulated by E. L. Thorndike was referred to as the law of
    A. associative shifting   B. recency
    C. exercise   D. readiness

    11.___

12. A high school teacher of economics in an academic high school tells you that almost half of the pupils in his senior year classes spend most of their time in his class daydreaming rather than participating in the class lesson. The *most promising* procedure for this teacher to follow is to
    A. refer these daydreaming pupils to the bureau of child guidance for intensive study
    B. realize that daydreaming is normal among adolescents
    C. base his lessons on economic problems confronting his pupils
    D. administer short surprise quizzes whenever inattention becomes widespread

    12.___

13. When classroom teachers attempt to deal with children's emotional difficulties which are at the basis of much serious misconduct, they *are inclined to*
    A. plan treatment programs which cover too long a period of time
    B. stress the removal of the cause rather than the elimination of annoying symptoms
    C. deal with immediate rather than basic causes of misconduct
    D. spend too much time assembling unnecessary data before they initiate their treatment program

    13.___

2. (#2)

8. Research has demonstrated that there is an increase in racial prejudice during adolescence. Of the following, the factor that contributes MOST significantly to this increase is
   A. dislike for deviants from norms of social groups
   B. influence of parental opinion
   C. segregation of groups in school and community
   D. fear of economic pressure from minority groups

9. When we compare young children and adolescents with respect to the relative effectiveness of distributed and concentrated practice as a learning technique we find that
   A. young children learn better by distributed practice; adolescents, by concentrated practice
   B. young children learn better by concentrated practice; adolescents, by distributed practice
   C. both young children and adolescents learn better by concentrated practice
   D. both young children and adolescents learn better by distributed practice

10. A child develops a headache every time a particularly distasteful task is announced. This type of reaction is characterized as
    A. hysterical   B. rationalization
    C. projection   D. physiological

11. The principle of the conditioned response as formulated by E. L. Thorndike was referred to as the law of
    A. associative shifting   B. recency
    C. exercise   D. readiness

12. A high school teacher of economics in an academic high school tells you that almost half of the pupils in his senior year classes spend most of their time in the class daydreaming rather than participating in the class lesson. The most promising procedure for this teacher to follow is to
    A. refer these daydreaming pupils to the bureau of child guidance for intensive study
    B. realize that daydreaming is normal among adolescents
    C. base his lessons on economic problems confronting his pupils
    D. administer short surprise quizzes whenever inattention becomes widespread

13. When classroom teachers attempt to deal with children's emotional difficulties which are at the basis of much serious misconduct, they are inclined to
    A. plan treatment programs which cover too long a period of time
    B. stress the removal of the cause rather than the elimination of annoying symptoms
    C. deal with immediate rather than basic cause of misconduct
    D. spend too much time assembling unnecessary data before they initiate their treatment program

14. The kind of elementary school boy who is *most likely* to be referred by a principal for study by a child guidance clinic is the pupil who
    A. misbehaves in the classroom
    B. does not have many close friendships with other children of his age
    C. is not interested in girls
    D. rarely volunteers in class

15. The program of elementary education, through its emphasis on learning by doing, is intended to make *what* use of intellectual processes?
    A. Stress them
    B. Include them
    C. Eliminate them
    D. Verbalize them

16. *Which one* of the following names is *NOT* associated with a reading readiness test?
    A. Gates   B. Gray   C. Metropolitan   D. Monroe

17. Bill's mother had been called to school because Bill's aggressive behavior has got him into disciplinary difficulties with his teacher. In speaking with the mother, the *FIRST* thing the teacher should attempt to do is to
    A. understand and respond to the feelings of the mother in the situation
    B. explain to the parent her responsibility for the child's behavior
    C. point out to the mother specifically which of her attitudes toward the boy needs changing
    D. propose suitable counseling agencies that might be consulted

18. Modern teaching of the mentally retarded *stresses*
    A. greater reliance upon memorization and a corresponding de-emphasis upon understanding
    B. closer correlation with life activities, including occupations
    C. re-education through emotional release and creative activities
    D. recognition that these children need the identical curriculum as the normal but require more time to master it

19. The unsociability often reported for very bright children is *most likely* to be due to
    A. their biological makeup
    B. their complete absorption in intellectual pursuits
    C. their lack of personal attractiveness
    D. the absence of suitable companions

20. *Which* of the following procedures would you expect to *INCREASE* the reliability of a test? Increasing the
    A. length of the test
    B. number of people tested
    C. number of types of items on the test
    D. homogeneity of the group tested

3. (#2)

14. The kind of elementary school boy who is most likely to be referred by a principal for study by a child guidance clinic is the pupil who
A. misbehaves in the classroom
B. does not have many close friendships with other children of his age
C. is not interested in girls
D. rarely volunteers in class

15. The program of elementary education, through its emphasis on learning by doing, is intended to make what use of intellectual processes?
A. Stress them   B. Include them
C. Eliminate them   D. Verbalize them

16. Which one of the following names is NOT associated with a reading readiness test?
A. Gates   B. Gray   C. Metropolitan   D. Monroe

17. Bill's mother had been called to school because Bill's aggressive behavior has got him into disciplinary difficulties with his teacher. In speaking with the mother, the FIRST thing the teacher should attempt to do is to
A. understand and respond to the feelings of the mother in the situation
B. explain to the parent her responsibility for the child's behavior
C. point out to the mother specifically which of her attitudes toward the boy needs changing
D. propose suitable counseling agencies that might be consulted

18. Modern teaching of the mentally retarded stresses
A. greater reliance upon memorization and a corresponding de-emphasis upon understanding
B. closer correlation with life activities, including occupations
C. re-education through emotional release and creative activities
D. recognition that these children need the identical curriculum as the normal but require more time to master it

19. The unsocial ability often reported for very bright children is more likely to be due to
A. their biological makeup
B. their complete absorption in intellectual pursuits
C. their lack of personal attractiveness
D. the absence of suitable companions

20. Which of the following procedures would you expect to INCREASE the reliability of a test? Increasing the
A. length of the test.   B. number of people tested
C. number of types of items on the test
D. homogeneity of the group tested

21. The Navy reports aptitude test results in terms of standard scores with a mean of 50 and a standard deviation of 10. A recruit with a mechanical comprehension score of 65 is a candidate for machinist training. On the basis of this score, he would be *judged*
    A. a very superior candidate
    B. likely to prove about average
    C. a borderline case
    D. a poor risk

22. A student fell at the 60th percentile on a 200-item final examination in biology given to his class of 80 pupils at school. This *means* that he
    A. was beaten by 48 pupils in the class
    B. was better than 48 pupils in the class
    C. got 120 items right
    D. was more than one standard deviation from the mean

23. For guidance work with senior high school students, one would find it *most generally* convenient to work with
    A. age norms   B. grade norms
    C. percentile norms   D. quotient norms

24. *If and when* a school system changes over to a 100% promotion plan, the need for special classes for mentally retarded pupils may be expected to
    A. become more evident as the range of scholastic ability within a single grade becomes greater
    B. apply to pupils entering the kindergarten as much as to pupils in the higher grades
    C. virtually disappear because of the elimination of school retardation and failure
    D. increase because of the need to place a larger proportion of intellectually normal but scholastically over-age pupils in special classes

25. Investigations have shown that in arithmetic the length of the practice period *generally* yielding greatest returns per period is
    A. 10 minutes   B. 30 minutes
    C. 45 minutes   D. 60 minutes

KEY (CORRECT ANSWERS)

1. B	6. A	11. A	16. B	21. A
2. D	7. C	12. C	17. A	22. B
3. D	8. A	13. C	18. B	23. C
4. A	9. D	14. A	19. D	24. A
5. A	10. A	15. B	20. A	25. C

21. The Navy reports aptitude test results in terms of standard scores with a mean of 50 and a standard deviation of 10. A recruit with a mechanical comprehension score of 65 is a candidate for machinist training. On the basis of this score, he would be judged
    A. a very superior candidate
    B. likely to prove about average
    C. a borderline case
    D. a poor risk

22. A student fell at the 60th percentile on a 200-item final examination in biology given to his class of 80 pupils at school. This means that he
    A. was beaten by 48 pupils in the class
    B. was better than 48 pupils in the class
    C. got 120 items right
    D. was more than one standard deviation from the mean

23. For guidance work with senior high school students, one would find most generally convenient to work with
    A. age norms   B. grade norms
    C. percentile norms   D. quotient norms

24. If and when a school system changes over to a 100% promotion plan, the need for special classes for mentally retarded pupils may be expected to
    A. become more evident as the range of scholastic ability within a single grade becomes greater
    B. apply to pupils entering the kindergarten as much as to pupils in the higher grades
    C. virtually disappear because of the elimination of school retardation as a feature
    D. increase because of the need to place a larger proportion of intellectually normal but scholastically over-age pupils in special classes

25. Investigations have shown that in arithmetic the length of the practice period generally yielding greatest returns per period is
    A. 10 minutes   B. 30 minutes
    C. 45 minutes   D. 60 minutes

KEY (CORRECT ANSWERS)

1. B	6. A	11. A	16. B	21. A
2. D	7. C	12. C	17. A	22. B
3. D	8. A	13. C	18. B	23. C
4. A	9. C	14. A	19. D	24. A
5. A	10. A	15. B	20. A	25. C

TEST 3

DIRECTIONS: Each question or incomplete statement is followed by several suggested answers or completions. Select the one that *BEST* answers the question or completes the statement. *PRINT THE LETTER OF THE CORRECT ANSWER IN THE SPACE AT THE RIGHT.*

1. *All* of the following are desirable educational practices EXCEPT
    A. starting the lesson promptly at the beginning of the period
    B. completing the lesson even if the class has to be detained a few minutes
    C. planning a motivation for each lesson
    D. eliciting the lesson aim from the pupils

2. Reinforcing learning can *BEST* be achieved when drill is
    A. given to all pupils regardless of achievement
    B. given in intensive doses
    C. individualized
    D. given without motivation

3. Thought-provoking answers are *most easily* achieved when
    A. a pupil's name is called before a question is asked
    B. a question is repeated several times in varied forms
    C. a question is asked and then a pupil is called upon to recite
    D. pupils anticipate the question

4. The teaching effectiveness of class discussions can be improved by all of the following EXCEPT having
    A. pupils face one another in speaking
    B. a competent recorder write main contributions on the blackboard
    C. the brighter pupils offer most of the contributions
    D. the group evaluate its own performance in terms of previously accepted objectives

5. A slow learner should be expected to do all of the following EXCEPT
    A. do brief written assignments
    B. work as hard as other pupils
    C. spend much of the day in manual art and fine art classes
    D. master a modified curriculum

6. In a science class where the majority of pupils have I.Q.'s lower than 85, *GREATEST* emphasis should be placed on *which one* of the following?
    A. Game - like activities for sensory-motor training
    B. Committee reports based on group research
    C. Drill and review activities
    D. Adaptation of subject matter to the interests and needs of the pupils

TEST 3

DIRECTIONS: Each question or incomplete statement is followed by several suggested answers or completions. Select the one that BEST answers the question or completes the statement. PRINT THE LETTER OF THE CORRECT ANSWER IN THE SPACE AT THE RIGHT.

1. All of the following are desirable educational practices EXCEPT
   A. starting the lesson promptly at the beginning of the period
   B. completing the lesson even if the class has to be detained a few minutes
   C. planning a motivation for each lesson
   D. eliciting the lesson aim from the pupils

2. Reinforcing learning can BEST be achieved when drill is
   A. given to all pupils regardless of achievement
   B. given in intensive doses
   C. individualized
   D. given without motivation

3. Thought-provoking answers are most easily achieved when
   A. a pupil's name is called before a question is asked
   B. a question is repeated several times in varied forms
   C. a question is asked and then a pupil is called upon to recite
   D. pupils anticipate the question

4. The teaching effectiveness of class discussions can be improved by all of the following EXCEPT having
   A. pupils face one another in speaking
   B. a competent recorder write main contributions on the blackboard
   C. the brighter pupils offer most of the contributions
   D. the group evaluate its own performance in terms of previously accepted objectives

5. A slow learner should be expected to do all of the following EXCEPT
   A. do brief written assignments
   B. work as hard as other pupils
   C. spend much of the day in manual art and fine art classes
   D. master a modified curriculum

6. In a science class where the majority of pupils have I.Q.'s lower than 85, GREATEST emphasis should be placed on which one of the following?
   A. Game-like activities for sensory-motor training
   B. Committee reports based on group research
   C. Drill and review activities
   D. Adaptation of subject matter to the interests and needs of the pupils

2. (#3)

7. In a science class, where the majority of pupils are retarded in reading, the *predominating* activity should be
   A. written work of one kind or another
   B. film and filmstrip lessons
   C. developmental lessons of various types
   D. phonics lessons based on the textbook

8. In a science class, the children's first-hand, out-of-school experiences should
   A. form the basis of the entire science course
   B. be supplemented and reinforced by the course of study
   C. constitute at least 50% of the science course
   D. be ignored if they have little direct relation to the course of study

9. Of the following possible questions for lessons in science, the *one* which BEST meets the criteria for a good teaching question is:
   I. Isn't it a fact that the stamen contains the anther?
   II. What about the piston?
   III. What is diastrophism and what theory is used to explain it?
   IV. Why do glaciers reach beyond the snow line?

   The CORRECT answer is:
   A. I   B. II   C. III   D. IV

10. *All* of the following items apply to the use of classroom demonstrations EXCEPT that the
    A. apparatus used should be as complex as possible
    B. demonstration should be visible to everyone in the room
    C. demonstration should be tried out in advance
    D. purpose of the demonstration should be clear

11. When a science teacher finds an unlabeled bottle containing a clear liquid in his storage cabinet, he should
    A. relabel it   B. discard it
    C. test it   D. give it to a student

12. A pupil has acid splashed on his face. The teacher washes the affected area and *then* should
    A. send the pupil home
    B. report the accident to the principal
    C. send for an ambulance
    D. call the parent on the phone

13. A test which measures that which it sets out to measure is said to be
    A. consistent   B. subjective   C. valid   D. reliable

14. Of the following, a technique that is *especially* useful for the study of inter-pupil relationships in a group or classroom situation is the
    A. anecdotal record   B. sociogram
    C. Rorschach Test   D. Thematic Apperception Test

2. (#3)

7. In a science class, where the majority of pupils are retarded in reading, the predominating activity should be
   A. written work of one kind or another
   B. film and filmstrip lessons
   C. developmental lessons of various types
   D. phonics lessons based on the textbook

8. In a science class, the children's first-hand, out-of-school experiences should
   A. form the basis of the entire science course
   B. be supplemented and reinforced by the course of study
   C. constitute at least 50% of the science course
   D. be ignored if they have little direct relation to the course of study

9. Of the following possible questions for lessons in science, the one which BEST meets the criteria for a good teaching question is:
   I. Isn't it a fact that the stamen contains the anthers?
   II. What about the piston?
   III. What is Catastrophism and what theory is used to explain it?
   IV. Why do glaciers reach beyond the snow line?

   The CORRECT answer is:
   A. I   B. II   C. III   D. IV

10. All of the following items apply to the use of classroom demonstrations EXCEPT that the
    A. apparatus used should be as complex as possible
    B. demonstration should be visible to everyone in the room
    C. demonstration should be tried out in advance
    D. purpose of the demonstration should be clear

11. When a science teacher finds an unlabeled bottle containing a clear liquid in his storage cabinet, he should
    A. relabel it   B. discard it
    C. test it   D. give it to a student

12. A pupil has acid splashed on his face. The teacher washes the affected area and then should
    A. send the pupil home
    B. report the student to the principal
    C. send for an ambulance
    D. call the parent on the phone

13. A test which measures that which it sets out to measure is said to be
    A. consistent   B. subjective   C. valid   D. reliable

14. Of the following, a technique that is especially useful for the study of inter-pupil relationships in a group or classroom situation is the
    A. anecdotal record   B. sociogram
    C. Rorschach Test   D. Thematic Apperception Test

15. A temporary psychological adjustment wherein one at- 15.___
tributes one's faults, weaknesses, and wishes to others
is called
   A. regression   B. projection
   C. repression   D. sublimation

16. If a pupil mispronounces a word, the teacher should 16.___
   A. ignore the error
   B. interrupt the recitation to correct the mispronunci-
      ation
   C. incidentally correct the error in an unobtrusive
      fashion
   D. give the pupil a lower mark

17. *All* of the following are objections to the use of punish- 17.___
    ment *EXCEPT*:
   A. The results of punishment are less predictable than
      the results of reward
   B. Punishment occasionally fixes the punished behavior
      rather than eliminates it
   C. The danger of injustice in punishment because of un-
      intended and disproportionate emotional upset is real
   D. Prompt punishment sometimes reduces anxiety by clarify-
      ing the limits for allowable behavior

18. The unit, "Our Atomic World," in a general science course 18.___
    of study, is *most likely* taught in
   A. Grade 7   B. Grade 8
   C. Grade 9   D. Grades 7, 8, and 9

19. The book SLUMS AND SUBURBS was written by 19.___
   A. Dr. James Conant   B. Admiral Hyman Rickover
   C. Commissioner Robert Moses
   D. Magistrate Anna Kross

20. Of the following periodicals, the *one* that is probably 20.___
    MOST difficult in regard to reading and maturity level
    for average junior high school science students is
   A. SCIENTIFIC AMERICAN   B. SCIENCE WORLD
   C. CURRENT SCIENCE AND AVIATION
   D. SCIENCE NEWS LETTER

21. Maintenance drills should be given 21.___
   A. to *all* pupils
   B. *only* to pupils studying algebra
   C. *only* to pupils who need remedial arithmetic
   D. *only* to pupils in the general mathematics classes

22. *Which one* of the following statements concerning skills 22.___
    and drills is *NOT* true?
   A. To maintain skills in mathematics, it is necessary to
      provide distributed practice of a variety of processes
   B. Traditionally, "drill" has meant the routine applica-
      tion of the law of "exercise" whereas "practice" in-
      volves repetition in a variety of situations
   C. Suitable provision must be made for helping the
      learner to be aware of his own progress
   D. All pupils in a class should be given the same drill
      in a given skill

15. A temporary psychological adjustment wherein one attributes one's faults, weaknesses, and wishes to others is called
    A. regression   B. projection
    C. repression   D. sublimation

16. If a pupil mispronounces a word, the teacher should
    A. ignore the error
    B. interrupt the recitation to correct the mispronunciation
    C. incidentally correct the error in an unobtrusive fashion
    D. give the pupil a lower mark

17. All of the following are objections to the use of punishment EXCEPT:
    A. The results of punishment are less predictable than the results of reward
    B. Punishment occasionally fixes the punished behavior rather than eliminates it
    C. The danger of injustice in punishment because of unintended and disproportionate emotional upset is real
    D. Prompt punishment sometimes reduces anxiety by clarifying the limits for allowable behavior

18. The unit, "Our Atomic World", in a general science course of study, is most likely taught in
    A. Grade 7   B. Grade 8
    C. Grade 9   D. Grades 7, 8, and 9

19. The book SLUMS AND SUBURBS was written by
    A. Dr. James Conant   B. Admiral Hyman Rickover
    C. Commissioner Robert Moss
    D. Magistrate Anna Kross

20. Of the following periodicals, the one that is probably most difficult in regard to reading and maturity level for average junior high school science students is
    A. SCIENTIFIC AMERICAN   B. SCIENCE WORLD
    C. CURRENT SCIENCE AND AVIATION
    D. SCIENCE NEWS LETTER

21. Maintenance drills should be given
    A. to all pupils
    B. only to pupils studying algebra
    C. only to pupils who need remedial arithmetic
    D. only to pupils in the general mathematics classes

22. Which one of the following statements concerning skills and drills is NOT true?
    A. To maintain skills in mathematics, it is necessary to provide distributed practice of a variety of processes
    B. Traditionally, "drill" has meant the routine application of the law of "exercise," whereas "practice" involves repetition in a variety of situations
    C. Suitable provision must be made for helping the learner to be aware of his own progress
    D. All pupils in a class should be given the same drill in a given skill

23. Of the following, the statement which is *NOT* descriptive of a characteristic of a *good* drill is that
    A. the exercises are graded
    B. understanding precedes the drill
    C. complex processes are emphasized
    D. the drill is addressed to pupil weaknesses

24. Tests should be given
    A. daily   B. at the completion of a unit
    C. without previous notice
    D. weekly

25. Of the following procedures, select the *one* which teachers should *NOT* use after having given the class a test in 9th year general mathematics:
    A. Return the marked test papers to all pupils
    B. Allow pupils to check and to discuss the test
    C. Note common errors which will be the basis of future lessons
    D. Drill the entire class on every error made by any student

---

KEY (CORRECT ANSWERS)

1.	B	11.	B
2.	C	12.	B
3.	C	13.	C
4.	C	14.	B
5.	C	15.	B
6.	D	16.	C
7.	C	17.	D
8.	B	18.	C
9.	D	19.	A
10.	A	20.	A

21. A
22. D
23. C
24. B
25. D

4. (W3)

23. Of the following, the statement which is NOT descriptive   23. ___
    of a characteristic of a good drill is that
    A. the exercises are graded
    B. understanding precedes the drill
    C. complex processes are emphasized
    D. the drill is addressed to pupil weaknesses

24. Tests should be given   24. ___
    A. daily   B. at the completion of a unit
    C. without previous notice
    D. weekly

25. Of the following procedures, select the one which   25. ___
    teachers should NOT use after having given the class
    a test in 9th year general mathematics:
    A. Return the marked test papers to all pupils
    B. Allow pupils to check and to discuss the test
    C. Note common errors which will be the basis of future
       lessons
    D. Drill the entire class on every error made by any
       student

———

KEY (CORRECT ANSWERS)

1. B   11. B
2. C   12. B
3. C   13. C
4. D   14. B
5. C   15. B

6. D   16. C
7. C   17. D
8. B   18. C
9. B   19. A
10. A   20. A

        21. A
        22. D
        23. C
        24. B
        25. D

———

TEST 4

DIRECTIONS: Each question or incomplete statement is followed by
several suggested answers or completions. Select the
one that *BEST* answers the question or completes the
statement. *PRINT THE LETTER OF THE CORRECT ANSWER IN
THE SPACE AT THE RIGHT.*

1. If a child enters a class late in the term, the teacher   1.___
    should
    A. replan her work
    B. fit the child into his skill achievement groups
       and continue with the social skills items the class
       is working on
    C. review all the work previously taught
    D. place child in a group by himself so as to best
       meet his individual needs

2. A progress chart for children *should show* each child   2.___
    competing with
    A. all the other children in the class
    B. his own record
    C. the children of his group
    D. all children with the same MA

3. Mary's father comes in to find out how she is doing in   3.___
    your class. Actually, Mary's work has become progressive-
    ly worse in the last few weeks. You should take this
    opportunity to
    A. encourage the father to help with her school work
       at home
    B. try to ascertain how Mary is adjusting at home
    C. show him examples of what Mary can do in comparison
       to other children
    D. dismiss Mary's weaknesses as relatively unimportant
       and stress her good points

4. The *MAJOR* barrier in the way of successful conferences   4.___
    between the teacher and parents is the
    A. hostile attitude of most of the parents
    B. lack of training on the part of the teacher in how
       to conduct an interview
    C. overzealousness on the part of the teacher to help
       her children
    D. problem of getting the parents to verbalize at such
       conferences

5. Of the following, the *MOST* important determinant of a   5.___
    favorable learning environment is the
    A. physical setting of the classroom
    B. course of study used
    C. interpersonal relationships in the classroom
    D. age range of the children

TEST 4

DIRECTIONS: Each question or incomplete statement is followed by several suggested answers or completions. Select the one that BEST answers the question or completes the statement. PRINT THE LETTER OF THE CORRECT ANSWER IN THE SPACE AT THE RIGHT.

1. If a child enters a class late in the term, the teacher should
   A. replan her work
   B. fit the child into his skill achievement groups and continue with the social skills items the class is working on
   C. review all the work previously taught
   D. place child in a group by himself so as to best meet his individual needs

   1.___

2. A progress chart for children should show each child competing with
   A. all the other children in the class
   B. his own record
   C. the children of his group
   D. all children with the same MA

   2.___

3. Mary's father comes in to find out how she is doing in your class. Actually, Mary's work has become progressively worse in the last few weeks. You should take this opportunity to
   A. encourage the father to help with her school work at home
   B. try to ascertain how Mary is adjusting at home
   C. show him examples of what Mary can do in comparison to other children
   D. dismiss Mary's weaknesses as relatively unimportant and stress her good points

   3.___

4. The MAJOR barrier in the way of successful conferences between the teacher and parents is the
   A. hostile attitude of most of the parents
   B. lack of training on the part of the teacher in how to conduct an interview
   C. overeagerness on the part of the teacher to help her children
   D. problem of getting the parents to verbalize at such conferences.

   4.___

5. Of the following, the MOST important determinant of a favorable learning environment is the
   A. physical setting of the classroom
   B. course of study used
   C. interpersonal relationships in the classroom
   D. age range of the children

   5.___

6. The teacher of a class can *BEST* motivate her pupils by having
   A. two groups of similar capabilities compete with each other
   B. individual students of similar capabilities compete with each other
   C. each student work at his own capacity, with rewards as incentives
   D. each student compete with himself

7. The *PRIMARY* factor the teacher should emphasize to speed up the acquisition of reading skills is the
   A. provision of a broad base of verbal experiences
   B. motivation of the pupils
   C. constant review of material
   D. use of the visual method in teaching reading

8. In learning situations, children are able to generalize most effectively when the principle to be abstracted is
   A. *embodied* in a single, clear, vivid and representative situation
   B. *repeated* in the same fashion numerous times
   C. *expressed* verbally by the teacher following many examples
   D. *repeated* in different settings and contexts

9. *In general*, the language development of girls is
   A. more rapid than that of boys
   B. less rapid than that of boys
   C. equal to that of boys
   D. more rapid than that of boys in oral communication, but slower in written communication

10. In the course of a conversation with the parent of a child in your class, she indicates that she "cannot understand why he is so stupid; his brothers and sisters all had good marks in school." You *should*
    A. ignore her references to the other children
    B. tell her that her attitude to the slow child is detrimental
    C. indicate how she may help the child at home
    D. tell her that her child will never measure up to his siblings

11. Defense mechanisms are used
    A. *most frequently* by average children
    B. *less frequently* by slow learners than by average children
    C. *more frequently* by slow learners than by average children
    D. *by all children* regardless of level of ability

12. Late yesterday afternoon, Michael, an 8-year-old child who had not given the teacher any trouble all term long, violently attacked another child in class for no apparent reason. The teacher should quell the disturbance *and*
    A. send him to the principal
    B. talk with him after class about the incident
    C. refer the case to child guidance specialists
    D. send a note home to his mother

2. (A4)

6. The teacher of a class can BEST motivate her pupils by having
   A. two groups of similar capabilities compete with each other
   B. individual students of similar capabilities compete with each other
   C. each student work at his own capacity, with rewards as incentives
   D. each student compete with himself

7. The PRIMARY factor the teacher should emphasize to speed up the acquisition of reading skills is the
   A. provision of a broad base of verbal experiences
   B. motivation of the pupils
   C. constant review of material
   D. use of the visual method in teaching reading

8. In learning situations, children are able to generalize most effectively when the principle is
   A. embodied in a single, clear, vivid and representative situation
   B. repeated in the same fashion numerous times
   C. expressed verbally by the teacher following many examples
   D. repeated in different settings and contexts

9. In general, the language development of girls is
   A. more rapid than that of boys
   B. less rapid than that of boys
   C. equal to that of boys
   D. more rapid than that of boys in oral communication, but slower in written communication

10. In the course of a conversation with the parent of a child in your class, she indicates that she "cannot understand why he is so stupid; his brothers and sisters all had good marks in school." You should
    A. ignore her references to the other children
    B. tell her that her attitude to the slow child is detrimental
    C. indicate how she may help the child at home
    D. tell her that her child will never measure up to his siblings

11. Defense mechanisms are used
    A. most frequently by average children
    B. less frequently by slow learners than by average children
    C. more frequently by slow learners than by average children
    D. by all children regardless of level of ability

12. Late yesterday afternoon, Michael, an 8-year-old child who had not given the teacher any trouble all term long, violently attacked another child in class for no apparent reason. The teacher should quell the disturbance and
    A. send him to the principal
    B. talk with him after class about the incident
    C. refer the case to child guidance specialists
    D. send a note home to his mother

13. John, a 10-year-old child, avoided his teacher during his first week in class. His behavior *most probably* reflects
    A. general attitudes developed in relation to authority figures
    B. guilt feelings over something he had done
    C. hostility which he was afraid to express
    D. natural cautionness shown by most children

14. Mrs. Jones related that recently, following the birth of a younger sister, her daughter Anne, an 8-year-old, began to have temper tantrums and to throw toys at the baby. In seeking to help the mother, the teacher should advise the mother to *impress upon* Anne that she
    A. should be as "good" as the baby
    B. has nothing to be jealous about
    C. will buy her some new toys if she behaves
    D. can be of great help in caring for the baby

15. Rationalization is characterized by
    A. excessive withdrawal from activity
    B. blaming another for one's own faults
    C. reasonable but not necessarily correct explanations for behavior
    D. excessive striving to make up for personal deficiencies

16. The *MOST* important factor contributing to the success of a therapeutic program with a seriously disturbed child is the
    A. mental ability of the child
    B. cooperation of parents and teachers in the therapeutic program
    C. relationship the therapist establishes with the child
    D. length of time which can be devoted to therapeutic work

17. Alfred and Bob are fraternal twins. Charles and Donald are identical twins. On the Stanford-Binet, Alfred and Donald both obtained IQ's of 70 while Bob obtained an IQ of 55. It is *most probable* that Charles will have a(n)
    A. higher IQ than Donald
    B. lower IQ than Bob
    C. lower IQ than Donald
    D. IQ that approximates Alfred's

18. In distinguishing between inherited mental deficiency and that acquired later in life, the *MOST* helpful information is obtained from a study of
    A. findings of psychogalvanometric examinations
    B. electroencephalograph results
    C. the incidence of deficiency in the family
    D. group intelligence test results

19. The *MOST* accurate measure of grade expectancy in reading is based upon
    A. standardized achievement test results
    B. previous academic achievement
    C. a measure of mental ability
    D. years of schooling

3. (#4)

13. John, a 10-year-old child, avoided his teacher during his first week in class. His behavior most probably reflects
    A. general attitudes developed in relation to authority figures.
    B. guilt feelings over something he had done.
    C. hostility which he was afraid to express
    D. natural cautiousness shown by most children

14. Mrs. Jones related that recently, following the birth of a younger sister, her daughter Anne, an 8-year-old, began to have temper tantrums and to throw toys at the baby. In seeking to help the mother, the teacher should advise the mother to impress upon Anne that she
    A. should be as "good" as the baby
    B. has nothing to be jealous about
    C. will buy her some new toys if she behaves
    D. can be of great help in caring for the baby

15. Rationalization is characterized by
    A. excessive withdrawal from activity
    B. blaming another for one's own faults
    C. reasonable but not necessarily correct explanations for behavior
    D. excessive striving to make up for personal deficiencies

16. The MOST important factor contributing to the success of a therapeutic program with a seriously disturbed child is the
    A. mental ability of the child
    B. cooperation of parents and teachers in the therapeutic program
    C. relationship the therapist establishes with the child
    D. length of time which can be devoted to therapeutic work

17. Alfred and Bob are fraternal twins. Charles and Donald are identical twins. On the Stanford-Binet, Alfred and Donald both obtained IQ's of 90 while Bob obtained an IQ of 95. It is most probable that Charles will have a(n)
    A. higher IQ than Donald.   B. lower IQ than Bob
    C. lower IQ than Donald
    D. IQ that approximates Alfred's

18. In distinguishing between inherited mental deficiency and that acquired later in life, the MOST helpful information is obtained from a study of
    A. findings of psychogalvanometric examinations
    B. electroencephalograph results
    C. the incidence of deficiency in the family
    D. group intelligence test results

19. The MOST accurate measure of grade expectancy in reading is based upon
    A. standardized achievement test results
    B. previous academic achievement
    C. a measure of mental ability
    D. years of schooling

20. In a class for adolescent children, it is observed that a negative correlation exists between CA and IQ. This *means* that
    A. there is no relationship between CA and IQ
    B. there is a negligible relationship between CA and IQ
    C. children with the higher CA's often have the higher IQ's
    D. children with the higher CA's often have the lower IQ's

21. Following the testing of an entire class in reading, the teacher notices that Philip obtained the median score of the class. This *means* that Philip
    A. exceeded 50% of the class
    B. obtained the mean score of the class
    C. obtained the highest class score
    D. obtained the lowest class score

22. In class, a sociogram indicates that 80% of the children choose John to sit next to. In *sociometric* language, he is the
    A. star   B. isolate   C. sociolite   D. protagonist

23. Susan exceeded 40% of her class in an arithmetic test. This *means* that she was
    A. in the lowest quartile of the class
    B. at the 40th percentile of the class
    C. at the 60th percentile of the class
    D. above the median of the group

24. A *SEVERE* reading disability exists when a child's record indicates that he is reading
    A. one year below average for his grade
    B. one year below average for his grade and age
    C. average for his grade but one year below average for his MA
    D. average for his MA but one year below average for his CA

25. Paints, shellacs, and turpentine are *preferably* kept
    A. in the custodian's office
    B. on a high shelf out of reach of the children
    C. in metal cabinets in the classroom
    D. under lock and key in the teacher's supply closet

KEY (CORRECT ANSWERS)

1. B	6. D	11. D	16. C	21. A
2. B	7. B	12. B	17. D	22. A
3. B	8. D	13. A	18. C	23. B
4. B	9. A	14. D	19. C	24. C
5. C	10. C	15. C	20. D	25. C

20. In a class for adolescent children, it is observed that a negative correlation exists between CA and IQ. This means that
A. there is no relationship between CA and IQ
B. there is a negligible relationship between CA and IQ
C. children with the higher CA's often have the higher IQ's
D. children with the higher CA's often have the lower IQ's

21. Following the testing of an entire class in reading, the teacher notices that Philip obtained the median score of the class. This means that Philip
A. exceeded 50% of the class
B. obtained the mean score of the class
C. obtained the highest class score
D. obtained the lowest class score

22. In class, a sociogram indicates that 80% of the children choose John to sit next to. In sociometric language, he is the
A. star   B. isolate   C. sociolite D. protagonist

23. Susan exceeded 40% of her class in an arithmetic test. This means that she was
A. in the lowest quartile of the class
B. at the 40th percentile of the class
C. at the 60th percentile of the class
D. above the median of the group

24. A SILVER reading disability exists when a child's record indicates that he is reading
A. one year below average for his grade
B. one year below average for his grade and age
C. average for his grade but one year below average for his MA
D. average for his MA but one year below average for his CA

25. Paints, shellacs, and turpentine are preferably kept
A. in the custodian's office
B. on a high shelf out of reach of the children
C. in metal cabinets in the classroom
D. under lock and key in the teacher's supply closet

KEY (CORRECT ANSWERS)

1. B	6. D	11. D	16. C	21. A
2. B	7. B	12. B	17. D	22. A
3. B	8. D	13. A	18. C	23. B
4. B	9. A	14. D	19. C	24. C
5. C	10. C	15. C	20. D	25. C

TEST 5

DIRECTIONS: Each question or incomplete statement is followed by several suggested answers or completions. Select the one that *BEST* answers the question or completes the statement. *PRINT THE LETTER OF THE CORRECT ANSWER IN THE SPACE AT THE RIGHT.*

1. I. Because of the American theory of separation of Church and State, it has become generally accepted that the public school should leave the teaching of moral values to the home and church.
   II. The United States Supreme Court has declared that religious instruction may be supervised by the public school authorities during released time so long as this instruction takes place away from the school.

   A. Both I and II are correct
   B. Both I and II are incorrect
   C. I is correct; II is incorrect
   D. I is incorrect; II is correct

   1.____

2. I. A child with visual or auditory deficiencies may be unaware of his condition even when the deficiency is quite marked.
   II. In the sixth grade it is appropriate and desirable to appoint a "window monitor" who will have the duty of adjusting the windows with a window pole from time to time.

   A. Both I and II are correct
   B. Both I and II are incorrect
   C. I is correct; II is incorrect
   D. I is incorrect; II is correct

   2.____

3. I. In fairness to other children, aggressive children should not be permitted more extensive use of materials than is allowed to other children.
   II. In grouping for reading instruction in the upper elementary school grades it is important to preserve mobility downwards as well as upwards.

   A. Both I and II are correct
   B. Both I and II are incorrect
   C. I is correct; II is incorrect
   D. I is incorrect; II is correct

   3.____

4. I. The basis for laziness and inattention may be largely physical, or it may lie in a poor home situation, or in an inadequate curriculum.
   II. Learning built on success following satisfying experiences is more enduring than that which is dissociated from natural interests.

   A. Both I and II are correct
   B. Both I and II are incorrect
   C. I is correct; II is incorrect
   D. I is incorrect; II is correct

   4.____

TEST 5

DIRECTIONS: Each question or incomplete statement is followed by several suggested answers or completions. Select the one that BEST answers the question or completes the statement. PRINT THE LETTER OF THE CORRECT ANSWER IN THE SPACE AT THE RIGHT.

1. I. Because of the American theory of separation of Church and State, it has become generally accepted that the public school should leave the teaching of moral values to the home and church.
   II. The United States Supreme Court has declared that religious instruction may be supervised by the public school authorities during released time so long as this instruction takes place away from the school.

   A. Both I and II are correct.
   B. Both I and II are incorrect.
   C. I is correct; II is incorrect.
   D. I is incorrect; II is correct.

1. _____

2. I. A child with visual or auditory deficiencies may be unaware of his condition even when the deficiency is quite marked.
   II. In the sixth grade it is appropriate and desirable to appoint a "window monitor" who will have the duty of adjusting the windows with a window pole from time to time.

   A. Both I and II are correct.
   B. Both I and II are incorrect.
   C. I is correct; II is incorrect.
   D. I is incorrect; II is correct.

2. _____

3. I. In fairness to other children, aggressive children should not be permitted more extensive use of materials than is allowed to other children.
   II. In grouping for reading instruction in the upper elementary school grades it is important to preserve mobility downwards as well as upwards.

   A. Both I and II are correct.
   B. Both I and II are incorrect.
   C. I is correct; II is incorrect.
   D. I is incorrect; II is correct.

3. _____

4. I. The basis for laziness and inattention may be largely physical, or it may lie in a poor home situation, or in an inadequate curriculum.
   II. Learning built on success following satisfying experiences is more enduring than that which is dissociated from natural interests.

   A. Both I and II are correct.
   B. Both I and II are incorrect.
   C. I is correct; II is incorrect.
   D. I is incorrect; II is correct.

4. _____

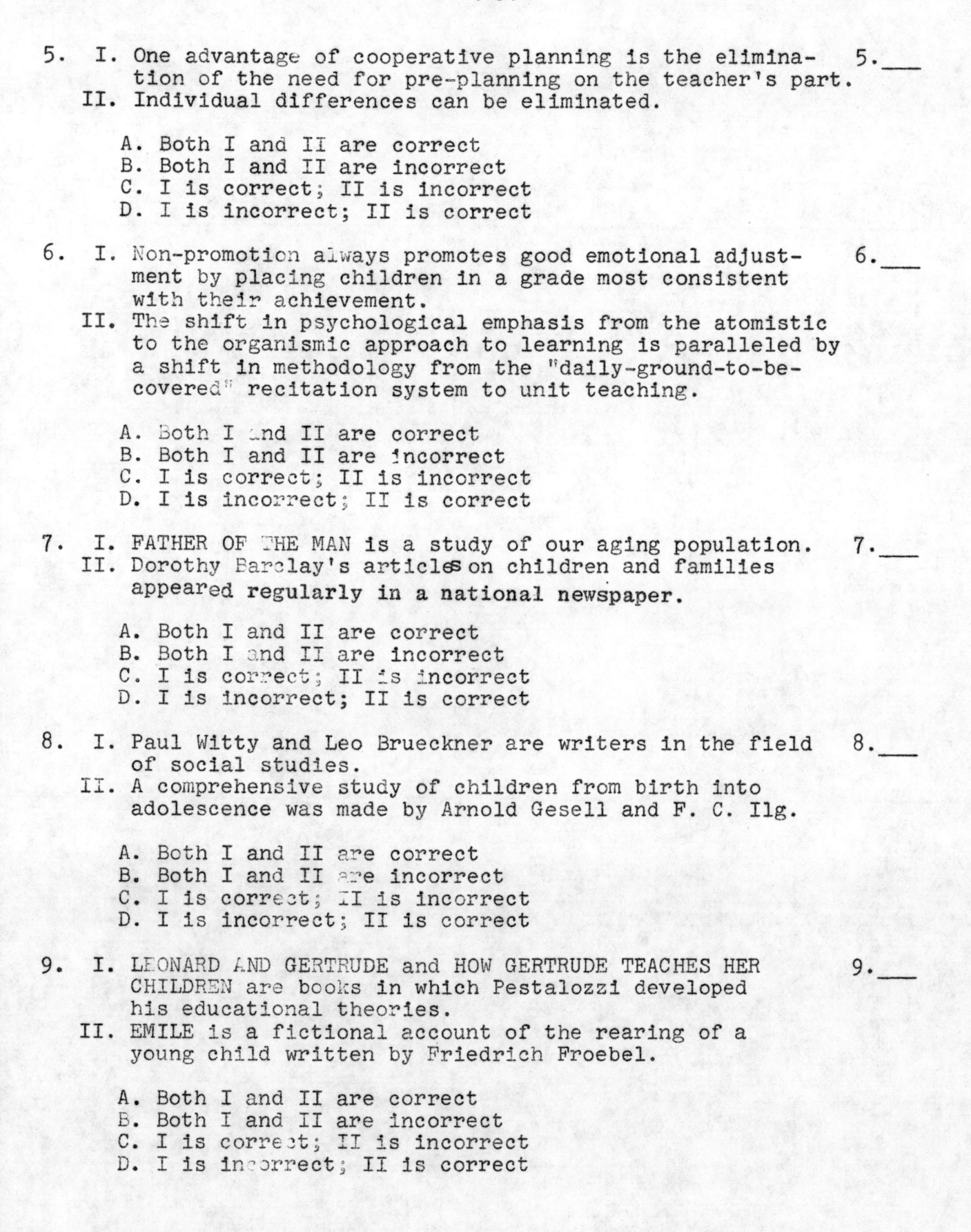

5. I. One advantage of cooperative planning is the elimination of the need for pre-planning on the teacher's part.
    II. Individual differences can be eliminated.

    A. Both I and II are correct
    B. Both I and II are incorrect
    C. I is correct; II is incorrect
    D. I is incorrect; II is correct

6. I. Non-promotion always promotes good emotional adjustment by placing children in a grade most consistent with their achievement.
    II. The shift in psychological emphasis from the atomistic to the organismic approach to learning is paralleled by a shift in methodology from the "daily-ground-to-be-covered" recitation system to unit teaching.

    A. Both I and II are correct
    B. Both I and II are incorrect
    C. I is correct; II is incorrect
    D. I is incorrect; II is correct

7. I. FATHER OF THE MAN is a study of our aging population.
    II. Dorothy Barclay's articles on children and families appeared regularly in a national newspaper.

    A. Both I and II are correct
    B. Both I and II are incorrect
    C. I is correct; II is incorrect
    D. I is incorrect; II is correct

8. I. Paul Witty and Leo Brueckner are writers in the field of social studies.
    II. A comprehensive study of children from birth into adolescence was made by Arnold Gesell and F. C. Ilg.

    A. Both I and II are correct
    B. Both I and II are incorrect
    C. I is correct; II is incorrect
    D. I is incorrect; II is correct

9. I. LEONARD AND GERTRUDE and HOW GERTRUDE TEACHES HER CHILDREN are books in which Pestalozzi developed his educational theories.
    II. EMILE is a fictional account of the rearing of a young child written by Friedrich Froebel.

    A. Both I and II are correct
    B. Both I and II are incorrect
    C. I is correct; II is incorrect
    D. I is incorrect; II is correct

2. (#5)

5. 1. One advantage of cooperative planning is the elimination of the need for pre-planning on the teacher's part.
II. Individual differences can be eliminated.

    A. Both I and II are correct.
    B. Both I and II are incorrect.
    C. I is correct; II is incorrect
    D. I is incorrect; II is correct

6. 1. Non-promotion always promotes good emotional adjustment by placing children in a grade most consistent with their achievement.
II. The shift in psychological emphasis from the atomistic to the organismic approach to learning is paralleled by a shift in methodology from the "daily-ground-to-be-covered" recitation system to unit teaching.

    A. Both I and II are correct.
    B. Both I and II are incorrect.
    C. I is correct; II is incorrect
    D. I is incorrect; II is correct

7. 1. FATHER OF THE MAN is a study of our aging population.
II. Dorothy Barclay's articles on children and families appeared regularly in a national newspaper.

    A. Both I and II are correct.
    B. Both I and II are incorrect.
    C. I is correct; II is incorrect
    D. I is incorrect; II is correct

8. 1. Paul Witty and Leo Brueckner are writers in the field of social studies.
II. A comprehensive study of children from birth into adolescence was made by Arnold Gesell and F. C. Ilg.

    A. Both I and II are correct.
    B. Both I and II are incorrect.
    C. I is correct; II is incorrect
    D. I is incorrect; II is correct

9. 1. LEONARD AND GERTRUDE and HOW GERTRUDE TEACHES HER CHILDREN are books in which Pestalozzi developed his educational theories.
II. EMILE is a fictional account of the rearing of a young child written by Friedrich Froebel.

    A. Both I and II are correct.
    B. Both I and II are incorrect.
    C. I is correct; II is incorrect
    D. I is incorrect; II is correct

10. I. William H. Kilpatrick is well known for his work in   10.___
       the field of Developmental Mathematics.
    II. Dr. A. B. Conant, formerly president of Harvary Uni-
        versity, then succeeded Dr. James Killian,
        president of Massachusetts Institute of Technology,
        as science advisor to the President of the United States.

    A. Both I and II are correct
    B. Both I and II are incorrect
    C. I is correct; II is incorrect
    D. I is incorrect; II is correct

11. I. A good teacher using the best possible classroom   11.___
       methods and procedures may sometimes fail to help
       poorly disciplined children to become better adjusted.
    II. If mathematical concepts are taught meaningfully in
        the elementary school, little, if any, drill is required.

    A. Both I and II are correct
    B. Both I and II are incorrect
    C. I is correct; II is incorrect
    D. I is incorrect; II is correct

12. I. A capable elementary school teacher can achieve   12.___
       integration among subject areas whatever the curriculum.
    II. Unique, or novel, methods can legitimately be used to
        reach traditional educational goals.

    A. Both I and II are correct
    B. Both I and II are incorrect
    C. I is correct; II is incorrect
    D. I is incorrect; II is correct

13. I. Recent studies of children have shown that the causes   13.___
       of maladjustment are much more frequently innate than
       environmental.
    II. A chief use of the sociogram is to measure achievement
        in the area of social studies.

    A. Both I and II are correct
    B. Both I and II are incorrect
    C. I is correct; II is incorrect
    D. I is incorrect; II is correct

14. I. The Puerto Rican child need not have as a goal pro-   14.___
       ficiency in reading and writing commensurate with that
       of native-born mainland children.
    II. An immediate goal of instruction of newly arrived
        Puerto Rican children is to develop understanding of
        and ability to use oral English.

    A. Both I and II are correct
    B. Both I and II are incorrect
    C. I is correct; II is incorrect
    D. I is incorrect; II is correct

3. (45).

10. I. William H. Kilpatrick is well known for his work in
    the field of Developmental Mathematics.
    II. Dr. A. B. Conant, formerly president of Harvard Uni-
    versity, then succeeded Dr. James Killian,
    president of Massachusetts Institute of Technology,
    as science Advisor to the President of the United States.

    A. Both I and II are correct.
    B. Both I and II are incorrect.
    C. I is correct; II is incorrect.
    D. I is incorrect; II is correct.

11. I. A good teacher using the best possible classroom
    methods and procedures may sometimes fail to help
    poorly disciplined children to become better adjusted.
    II. If mathematical concepts are taught meaningfully in
    the elementary school, little, if any, drill is required.

    A. Both I and II are correct.
    B. Both I and II are incorrect.
    C. I is correct; II is incorrect.
    D. I is incorrect; II is correct.

12. I. A capable elementary school teacher can achieve
    integration among subject areas whatever the curriculum.
    II. Unique, or novel, methods can legitimately be used to
    reach traditional educational goals.

    A. Both I and II are correct.
    B. Both I and II are incorrect.
    C. I is correct; II is incorrect.
    D. I is incorrect; II is correct.

13. I. Recent studies of children have shown that the causes
    of maladjustment are much more frequently innate than
    environmental.
    II. A chief use of the sociogram is to measure achievement
    in the area of social studies.

    A. Both I and II are correct.
    B. Both I and II are incorrect.
    C. I is correct; II is incorrect.
    D. I is incorrect; II is correct

14. I. The Puerto Rican child need not have as a goal pro-
    ficiency in reading and writing commensurate with that
    of native-born mainland children.
    II. An immediate goal of instruction of newly arrived
    Puerto Rican children is to develop understanding of
    and ability to use oral English.

    A. Both I and II are correct.
    B. Both I and II are incorrect.
    C. I is correct; II is incorrect.
    D. I is incorrect; II is correct.

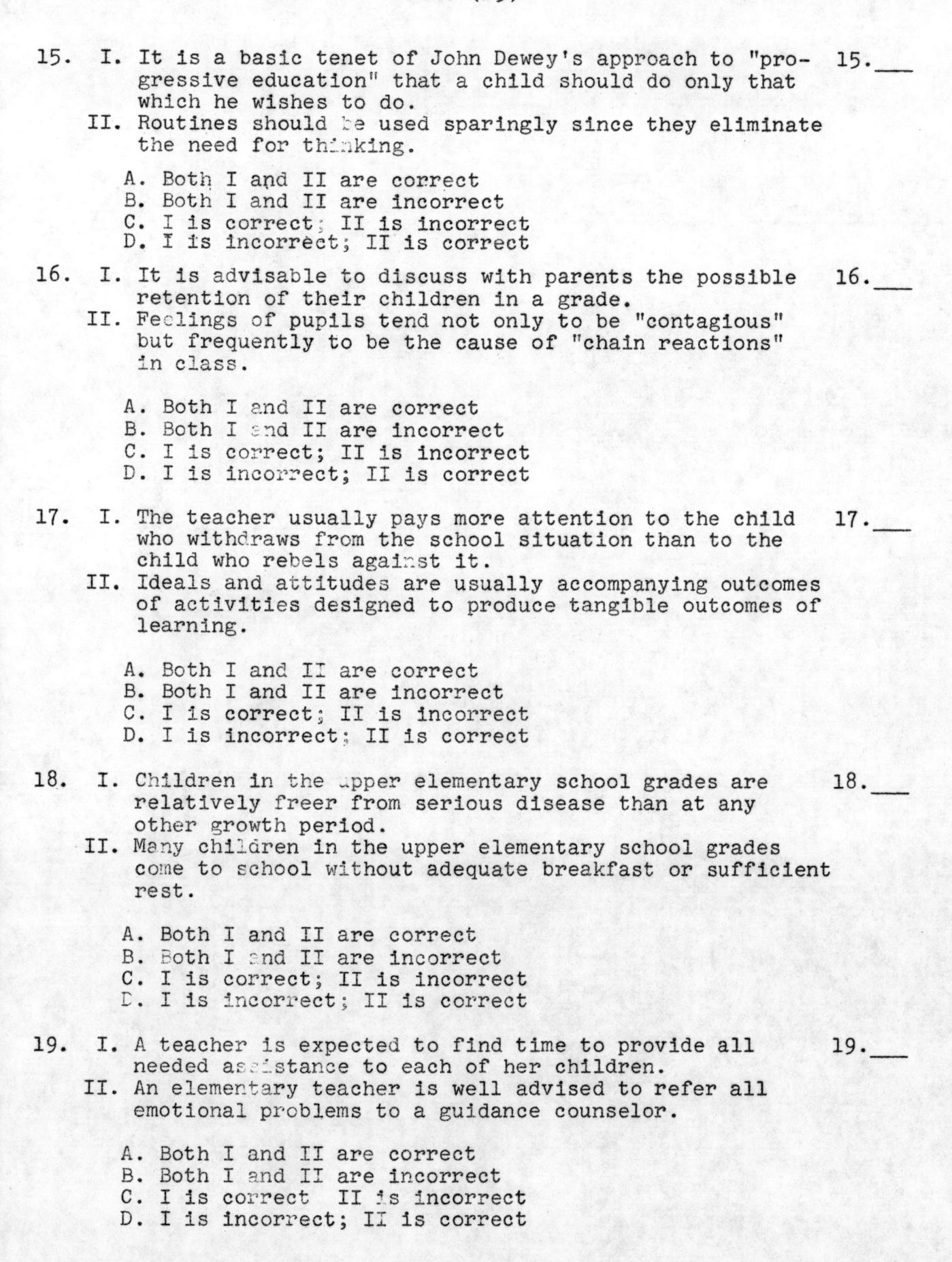

15. I. It is a basic tenet of John Dewey's approach to "progressive education" that a child should do only that which he wishes to do.
    II. Routines should be used sparingly since they eliminate the need for thinking.

    A. Both I and II are correct
    B. Both I and II are incorrect
    C. I is correct; II is incorrect
    D. I is incorrect; II is correct

15.___

16. I. It is advisable to discuss with parents the possible retention of their children in a grade.
    II. Feelings of pupils tend not only to be "contagious" but frequently to be the cause of "chain reactions" in class.

    A. Both I and II are correct
    B. Both I and II are incorrect
    C. I is correct; II is incorrect
    D. I is incorrect; II is correct

16.___

17. I. The teacher usually pays more attention to the child who withdraws from the school situation than to the child who rebels against it.
    II. Ideals and attitudes are usually accompanying outcomes of activities designed to produce tangible outcomes of learning.

    A. Both I and II are correct
    B. Both I and II are incorrect
    C. I is correct; II is incorrect
    D. I is incorrect; II is correct

17.___

18. I. Children in the upper elementary school grades are relatively freer from serious disease than at any other growth period.
    II. Many children in the upper elementary school grades come to school without adequate breakfast or sufficient rest.

    A. Both I and II are correct
    B. Both I and II are incorrect
    C. I is correct; II is incorrect
    D. I is incorrect; II is correct

18.___

19. I. A teacher is expected to find time to provide all needed assistance to each of her children.
    II. An elementary teacher is well advised to refer all emotional problems to a guidance counselor.

    A. Both I and II are correct
    B. Both I and II are incorrect
    C. I is correct II is incorrect
    D. I is incorrect; II is correct

19.___

4. (#5)

15. I. It is a basic tenet of John Dewey's approach to "pro- 15. ___
gressive education, that a child should do only that
which he wishes to do.
II. Routines should be used sparingly since they eliminate
the need for thinking.

    A. Both I and II are correct.
    B. Both I and II are incorrect
    C. I is correct, II is incorrect
    D. I is incorrect, II is correct

16. I. It is advisable to discuss with parents the possible 16. ___
retention of their children in a grade.
II. Feelings of pupils tend not only to be "contagious"
but frequently to be the cause of "chain reactions"
in class.

    A. Both I and II are correct
    B. Both I and II are incorrect
    C. I is correct, II is incorrect
    D. I is incorrect; II is correct

17. I. The teacher usually pays more attention to the child 17. ___
who withdraws from the school situation than to the
child who rebels against it.
II. Ideals and attitudes are usually accompanying outcomes
of activities designed to produce tangible outcomes of
learning.

    A. Both I and II are correct
    B. Both I and II are incorrect
    C. I is correct, II is incorrect
    D. I is incorrect; II is correct

18. I. Children in the upper elementary school grades are 18. ___
relatively free from serious disease than at any
other growth period.
II. Many children in the upper elementary school grades
come to school without adequate breakfast or sufficient
rest.

    A. Both I and II are correct.
    B. Both I and II are incorrect.
    C. I is correct; II is incorrect
    D. I is incorrect; II is correct

19. I. A teacher is expected to find time to provide all 19. ___
needed assistance to each of her children.
II. An elementary teacher is well advised to refer all
emotional problems to a guidance counselor.

    A. Both I and II are correct
    B. Both I and II are incorrect
    C. I is correct, II is incorrect
    D. I is incorrect; II is correct

5. (#5)

20. I. One of the major activities of curriculum development 20.___
    in the nineteenth century consisted of observing the
    patterns in Europe and adopting them to our purposes
    and circumstances.
    II. No less an authority than John Dewey said that "up
    to the present time the weakest point in progressive
    schools is in the matter of selection and organization
    of intellectual subject matter."

    A. Both I and II are correct
    B. Both I and II are incorrect
    C. I is correct; II is incorrect
    D. I is incorrect; II is correct

21. I. The well-known American educator who wrote HOW WE 21.___
    THINK also wrote THE PROJECT METHOD.
    II. THE CHILD FROM FIVE TO TEN was written by Arnold Gesell
    and Frances Ilg.

    A. Both I and II are correct
    B. Both I and II are incorrect
    C. I is correct; II is incorrect
    D. I is incorrect; II is correct

22. I. Horace Mann was a pioneer in the development of the 22.___
    American public school
    II. Edward L. Thorndike is recognized as one of the out-
    standing authorities on the history of education in
    the United States.

    A. Both I and II are correct
    B. Both I and II are incorrect
    C. I is correct; II is incorrect
    D. I is incorrect; II is correct

23. I. The theory of the five steps in teaching: preparation, 23.___
    presentation, association, generalization and applica-
    tion, is most closely associated with Comenius.
    II. Although the works of Pestalozzi, Herbart and Froebel
    were well known in 19th Century Europe, they had little
    effect on education in the United States.

    A. Both I and II are correct
    B. Both I and II are incorrect
    C. I is correct; II is incorrect
    D. I is incorrect; II is correct

24. I. William H. Kilpatrick has achieved renown chiefly in 24.___
    the field of mental hygiene and child development.
    II. Arthur Gates and William Gray are well known among
    educators for their work in the teaching of science.

    A. Both I and II are correct
    B. Both I and II are incorrect
    C. I is correct; II is incorrect
    D. I is incorrect; II is correct

5. (45)

20. I. One of the major activities of curriculum development in the nineteenth century consisted of observing the patterns in Europe and adapting them to our purposes and other stances.
II. No less an authority than John Dewey said that "up to the present time the weakest point in progressive schools is in the matter of selection and organization of intellectual subject matter."

    A. Both I and II are correct
    B. Both I and II are incorrect
    C. I is correct; II is incorrect
    D. I is incorrect; II is correct

21. I. The well-known American educator who wrote HOW WE THINK also wrote THE PROJECT METHOD.
II. THE CHILD FROM FIVE TO TEN was written by Arnold Gesell and Frances Ilg.

    A. Both I and II are correct
    B. Both I and II are incorrect
    C. I is correct; II is incorrect
    D. I is incorrect; II is correct

22. I. Horace Mann was a pioneer in the development of the American public school
II. Edward L. Thorndike is recognized as one of the outstanding authorities on the history of education in the United States.

    A. Both I and II are correct
    B. Both I and II are incorrect
    C. I is correct; II is incorrect
    D. I is incorrect; II is correct

23. I. The theory of the five steps in teaching: preparation, presentation, association, generalization and application, is most closely associated with Comenius.
II. Although the works of Pestalozzi, Herbart and Froebel were well known in 19th Century Europe, they had little effect on education in the United States.

    A. Both I and II are correct
    B. Both I and II are incorrect
    C. I is correct; II is incorrect
    D. I is incorrect; II is correct

24. I. William H. Kilpatrick has achieved renown chiefly in the field of mental hygiene and child development.
II. Arthur Gates and William Gray are well known among educators for their work in the teaching of science.

    A. Both I and II are correct
    B. Both I and II are incorrect
    C. I is correct; II is incorrect
    D. I is incorrect; II is correct

5. (#5)

20. I. One of the major activities of curriculum development 20.___
    in the nineteenth century consisted of observing the
    patterns in Europe and adopting them to our purposes
    and circumstances.
    II. No less an authority than John Dewey said that "up
    to the present time the weakest point in progressive
    schools is in the matter of selection and organization
    of intellectual subject matter."

    A. Both I and II are correct
    B. Both I and II are incorrect
    C. I is correct; II is incorrect
    D. I is incorrect; II is correct

21. I. The well-known American educator who wrote HOW WE 21.___
    THINK also wrote THE PROJECT METHOD.
    II. THE CHILD FROM FIVE TO TEN was written by Arnold Gesell
    and Frances Ilg.

    A. Both I and II are correct
    B. Both I and II are incorrect
    C. I is correct; II is incorrect
    D. I is incorrect; II is correct

22. I. Horace Mann was a pioneer in the development of the 22.___
    American public school
    II. Edward L. Thorndike is recognized as one of the out-
    standing authorities on the history of education in
    the United States.

    A. Both I and II are correct
    B. Both I and II are incorrect
    C. I is correct; II is incorrect
    D. I is incorrect; II is correct

23. I. The theory of the five steps in teaching: preparation, 23.___
    presentation, association, generalization and applica-
    tion, is most closely associated with Comenius.
    II. Although the works of Pestalozzi, Herbart and Froebel
    were well known in 19th Century Europe, they had little
    effect on education in the United States.

    A. Both I and II are correct
    B. Both I and II are incorrect
    C. I is correct; II is incorrect
    D. I is incorrect; II is correct

24. I. William H. Kilpatrick has achieved renown chiefly in 24.___
    the field of mental hygiene and child development.
    II. Arthur Gates and William Gray are well known among
    educators for their work in the teaching of science.

    A. Both I and II are correct
    B. Both I and II are incorrect
    C. I is correct; II is incorrect
    D. I is incorrect; II is correct

20. I. One of the major activities of curriculum development in the nineteenth century consisted of observing the patterns in Europe and adapting them to our purposes and other stages.
II. No less an authority than John Dewey said that "up to the present time the weakest point in progressive schools is in the matter of selection and organization of intellectual subject matter.

    A. Both I and II are correct.
    B. Both I and II are incorrect
    C. I is correct; II is incorrect
    D. I is incorrect; II is correct

21. I. The well-known American educator who wrote HOW WE THINK also wrote THE PROJECT METHOD.
II. THE CHILD FROM FIVE TO TEN was written by Arnold Gesell and Frances Ilg.

    A. Both I and II are correct.
    B. Both I and II are incorrect.
    C. I is correct; II is incorrect
    D. I is incorrect; II is correct

22. I. Horace Mann was a pioneer in the development of the American public school
II. Edward L. Thorndike is recognized as one of the outstanding authorities on the history of education in the United States.

    A. Both I and II are correct.
    B. Both I and II are incorrect
    C. I is correct; II is incorrect
    D. I is incorrect; II is correct

23. I. The theory of the five steps in teaching: preparation, presentation, association, generalization and application, is most closely associated with Comenius.
II. Although the works of Pestalozzi, Herbart and Froebel were well known in 19th Century Europe, they had little effect on education in the United States.

    A. Both I and II are correct.
    B. Both I and II are incorrect
    C. I is correct; II is incorrect
    D. I is incorrect; II is correct

24. I. William H. Kilpatrick has achieved renown chiefly in the field of mental hygiene and child development.
II. Arthur Gates and William Gray are well known among educators for their work in the teaching of science.

    A. Both I and II are correct.
    B. Both I and II are incorrect
    C. I is correct; II is incorrect
    D. I is incorrect; II is correct

6. (#5)

25. I. Conant and Morton are generally recognized as authorities on the teaching of science.
    II. John Dewey's work in the area of progressive education has been furthered and favorably interpreted by Arthur Bestor.

    A. Both I and II are correct
    B. Both I and II are incorrect
    C. I is correct; II is incorrect
    D. I is incorrect; II is correct

25.___

KEY   (CORRECT ANSWERS)

1. B
2. C
3. D
4. A
5. B

6. D
7. B
8. D
9. C
10. B

11. C
12. A
13. B
14. D
15. B

16. A
17. D
18. A
19. B
20. A

21. D
22. C
23. B
24. B
25. C

---

25. I. Conant and Morton are generally recognized as au-
    thorities on the teaching of science.
    II. John Dewey's work in the area of progressive educa-
    tion has been furthered and favorably interpreted by
    Arthur Bestor.

    A. Both I and II are correct.
    B. Both I and II are incorrect.
    C. I is incorrect; II is incorrect.
    D. I is incorrect; II is correct.

KEY (CORRECT ANSWERS)

1. B	11. C
2. C	12. A
3. D	13. B
4. A	14. D
5. B	15. B
6. D	16. A
7. D	17. D
8. D	18. A
9. C	19. B
10. B	20. A

21. D
22. C
23. B
24. B
25. C

EXAMINATION SECTION

TEST 1

Questions 1-20.

DIRECTIONS: In each of the following groups, one sentence contains an underlined word which make the sentence INCORRECT. Select this sentence and indicate your choice on the answer sheet.

1. A. This assignment is so easy that many regard it as a <u>sinecure</u>.
   B. The decision was considered <u>parochial</u> because of its universal implications.
   C. Your generosity indicates you are a <u>magnanimous</u> man.
   D. Two students were injured during the <u>fracas</u>.

2. A. Arizona's dry climate is considered <u>salutary</u> for people suffering from respiratory ailments.
   B. Noting the <u>mitigating</u> circumstances, the judge suspended sentence.
   C. Many atrocities were committed by the <u>barbarous</u> tribes.
   D. The speaker's <u>banal</u> remarks generated considerable enthusiasm in the audience.

3. A. His speech was so <u>impassioned</u> as to transmit his emotion to all of his listeners.
   B. Allied to the domesticated llama and alpaca, the <u>lacuna</u> is a wild creature of the Andes.
   C. His speech was of <u>pedestrian</u> quality; it moved no one in the audience.
   D. I may be frugal, but I am not <u>parsimonious</u>.

4. A. The choice of leader was decided by a <u>plebiscite</u>.
   B. The manager was a master of evasiveness and <u>dissimulation</u>.
   C. Unsheathing his <u>shibboleth</u>, the warrior advanced warily.
   D. Wine and song added to the <u>conviviality</u> of the occasion.

5. A. So soothing was the <u>emolument</u> applied to the wound that the pain abated almost <u>instantly</u>.
   B. In view of the culprit's extreme youth, the jury recommended <u>clemency</u>.
   C. Oliver Twist soon found himself using the <u>argot</u> of thieves and rogues.
   D. Because of his glorification of the British soldier, Kipling was frequently labeled <u>chauvinistic</u>.

6. A. The signed <u>deposition</u> of the witness was accepted as evidence.
   B. Today, one would hardly regard the banana as an <u>exotic</u> fruit.
   C. Much of the holiday oratory is <u>vacuous</u> and designed mostly to fill time.
   D. Many people believe that some combinations of food, such as pickles and ice cream, are incompatible and <u>indigenous</u>.

TEST I

Questions 1-20.

DIRECTIONS: In each of the following groups, one sentence contains
an underlined word which make the sentence INCORRECT.
Select this sentence and indicate your choice on the
answer sheet.

1. A. This assignment is so easy that many regard it as a sinecure.
   B. The decision was considered parochial because of its universal
      implications.
   C. Your generosity indicates you are a magnanimous man.
   D. Two students were injured during the fracas.

2. A. Arizona's dry climate is considered salutary for people suf-
      fering from respiratory ailments.
   B. Noting the mitigating circumstances, the judge suspended
      sentence.
   C. Many atrocities were committed by the barbarous tribes.
   D. The speaker's banal remarks repeated considerable enthusiasm
      in the audience.

3. A. His speech was so impassioned as to transmit his emotion to all
      of his listeners.
   B. Allied to the domesticated llama and alpaca, the lacuna is a
      wild creature of the Andes.
   C. His speech was of pedestrian quality; it moved no one in the
      audience.
   D. I may be frugal, but I am not parsimonious.

4. A. The choice of leader was decided by a plebiscite.
   B. The manager was a master of evasiveness and prevarication.
   C. Unsheathing his shibboleth, the warrior advanced warily.
   D. Wine and song added to the conviviality of the occasion.

5. A. So soothing was the emolument applied to the wound that the
      pain abated almost instantly.
   B. In view of the culprit's extreme youth, the jury recommended
      clemency.
   C. Oliver Twist soon found himself amidst the argot of thieves
      and rogues.
   D. Because of his glorification of the British soldier, Kipling
      was frequently labeled chauvinistic.

6. A. The signed deposition of the witness was accepted as evidence.
   B. Today, one could hardly regard the banana as an exotic fruit.
   C. Much of the holiday oratory is vacuous and designed mostly to
      kill time.
   D. Many people believe that some combinations of food, such as
      pickles and ice cream, are incompatible and indigenous.

7. A. Ulysses' wanderings were not desultory they followed a pre-destined pattern.
   B. The French are noted for their gourmet dishes; their patois, cooked with rare herbs, is a good example.
   C. A spate of words gushed from the orator's lips.
   D. The F.B.I. found evidence of sabotage in the train wreck.

8. A. It had all the impetus of the first rush of a torrent.
   B. The lion is a predatory animal.
   C. Preferring to remain anomalous, the philanthropist did not divulge his name.
   D. A Utopian is one who hopes for a state of perfection in society.

9. A. The ubiquitous billboard, appearing at every turn, has despoiled our highways.
   B. The lesson in the orthography of English emphasized the non-phonetic character of the language.
   C. It is only in the last stage of metamorphosis that the butterfly becomes attractive.
   D. The medieval clergy were distinguished by the rich vestiges which they wore on all important occasions.

10. A. He delivered an urbane and witty speech that reflected his great sophistication.
    B. The meanderings of the river proved to be the most beautiful if not the shortest route to town.
    C. His native shrewdness and a general lack of ethics often caused him to circumspect the rules.
    D. The presumption of innocence until proven guilty is a cornerstone of our legal system.

11. A. It was difficult to reason with the politician because of his intransigent personality.
    B. The pupil's writing contained many egregious errors in grammar and usage.
    C. The nations of the world have an unprecedented opportunity to establish peace.
    D. Because Michael's veracity was well-known, his word was never doubted.

12. A. Many extremely intelligent people display ingenousness when faced with business decisions.
    B. The entomologist specialized in the study of the origins of the Sanskrit language.
    C. Their agreement was abrogated by mutual consent.
    D. Mark Antony exhorted the masses to seek revenge for Caesar's death.

13. A. His failure to enter extra-curricular activities arose from an inborn temerity which made him hesitant to volunteer.
    B. Although many specimens of Confederate money have considerable value, much of it is completely nugatory.
    C. New Englanders are reputed to be laconic in speech, rarely wasting a word.
    D. The enigmatic language of much modern poetry requires close analysis by the reader to determine meaning.

7. A. Ulysses' wanderings were not desultory; they followed a pre-
      determined pattern.
   B. The French are noted for their former, dapper, their patrons
      cocked at a cute angle, in a good example.
   C. A spate of words passed from the orator's lips.
   D. The F.B.I. found evidence of sabotage in the train wreck.

8. A. It had all the impetus of the fleet rush of a torrent.
   B. The lion is a tragedian of the N.
   C. Preferring to remain anonymous, the philanthropist did not
      divulge his name.
   D. A Utopian is one who hopes for a state of perfection in society.

9. A. The Chinitzca billboard, appearing at every turn, has despoiled
      our highways.
   B. The lesson in the orthography of English emphasized the mor-
      phemic character of the language.
   C. It is only in the last stage of metamorphosis that the butter-
      fly becomes attractive.
   D. The medieval clergy were distinguished by the rich vestiges
      which they wore on all important occasions.

10. A. He delivered an inspiring and witty speech that reflected his great
       sophistication.
    B. Nothing is sadder than a child who finds he is in poor health
       if not the happiest hours to come.
    C. Native shrewdness and a general lack of ethics often caused
       him to circumvent the rules.
    D. The presumption of innocence until proven guilty is a corner-
       stone of our legal system.

11. A. It was difficult to reason with the polite man because of his
       intense stubbornness.
    B. The pupil's writing contained many egregious errors in grammar
       and usage.
    C. The nations of the world saw an unprecedented opportunity to
       establish peace.
    D. Because Michael's veracity was well-known, his word was never
       doubted.

12. A. Many extremely intelligent people display an impassiveness when
       faced with thankless decisions.
    B. The authority of specialized in the study of the origins of
       the Egyptian language.
    C. Their agreement was approved by mutual consent.
    D. Mark Antony expressed the desire to seek revenge for Caesar's
       death.

13. A. His failure to enter extra-curricular activities stems from an
       inborn tenacity which made him hesitant to volunteer.
    B. Although many specimens of Confederate money have considerable
       value, much of it is completely useless.
    C. Few Hyzlaists are inclined to be laconic in speech, rarely
       wasting a word.
    D. The enigmatic language of much modern poetry requires close
       analysis by the reader to determine meaning.

14. A. A fire in a home at night creates conditions of such exigency that the residents must take immediate steps to save themselves.
    B. The natives of the island attacked the enemy with a shower of epistles from the trees.
    C. The union of chemical compounds or elements to form another compound is an example of synthesis.
    D. Many plants do not put forth leaves in winter because these plants are dormant at that time.

15. A. It is expected that the legislature will rescind the objectionable law.
    B. While this is an excellent medicine, it is by no means a panacea.
    C. His remarks were caustic and bitter, rather in the nature of persiflage.
    D. With cajolery and blandishment he finally inveigled his friend into joining in the venture.

16. A. Even the most honorable candidate for office may be maligned by his opponents.
    B. The mendicant pleaded for alms in a whining voice.
    C. Hannibal was a master of military strategy and logistics.
    D. Any encomium may be regarded as a form of slander.

17. A. An unfortunate juxtaposition of numerals caused the error in addition.
    B. Except for a superfluity of words, the thesis was well worth reading.
    C. Dancing and smoking are proscribed by certain religious sects.
    D. The tourists admired the simple, unpretentious forms of the baroque architecture.

18. A. The fearless hunter could not escape the tenuous grip of the savage beast.
    B. A person has to inure himself to the hardships of life.
    C. The audience was enthralled by the beauty and majesty of the music.
    D. When the president was introduced, pandemonium broke out.

19. A. Narcotics are often used to palliate excruciating pain.
    B. The wife took advantage of her husband's uxorious nature.
    C. The lieutenant was endowed with great courage.
    D. His reticence in accepting the office was indicative of his enthusiastic, ebullient personality.

20. A. We were almost suffocated by the acrid smells.
    B. The lascivious books were confiscated.
    C. The captain was honored for his craven behavior in the bloody campaign.
    D. The new drug was extolled by members of the medical profession

14. A. A fire in a home at night creates conditions of such exigency that the residents must take immediate steps to save themselves.
    B. The natives of the island attacked the enemy with a shower of splinters from the trees.
    C. The union of chemical compounds or elements to form another compound is an example of synthesis.
    D. Many plants do not put forth leaves in winter because these plants are dormant at that time.

15. A. It is expected that the legislature will rescind the objectionable law.
    B. While this is an excellent medicine, it is by no means a panacea.
    C. His remark was caustic and bitter, rather in the nature of persiflage.
    D. With cajolery and blandishment he finally inveigled his friend into joining in the venture.

16. A. Even the most honorable candidate for office may be maligned by his opponents.
    B. The mendicant pleaded for alms in a whining voice.
    C. Hannibal was a master of military strategy and logistics.
    D. Any encomium may be regarded as a form of slander.

17. A. An unfortunate juxtaposition of numerals caused the error in addition.
    B. Insofar as a superficiality of words, the thesis was well worth reading.
    C. Laxality and smoking are proscribed by certain religious sects.
    D. Fanaticism displays the simple, uncomplicated forms of the human reactions.

18. A. The fearless hunter could not escape the tenuous grip of the ravage beast.
    B. A person has to inure himself to the hardships of life.
    C. The audience was enthralled by the beauty and majesty of the music.
    D. When the president was introduced, pandemonium broke out.

19. A. Narcotics are often used to palliate excruciating pain.
    B. The wife took advantage of her husband's uxorious nature.
    C. The lieutenant was endowed with great courage.
    D. His reticence in accepting the office was indicative of his own domestic, emulient personality.

20. A. He was almost suffocated by the acrid smells.
    B. The lascivious books were confiscated.
    C. The captain was honored for his craven behavior in the bloody campaign.
    D. The new drug was extolled by members of the medical profession

Questions 21-35.

DIRECTIONS: In each of the following groups of sentences, one of the four sentences is faulty in capitalization, punctuation, grammar, spelling, sentence structure, diction, etc. Select the INCORRECT sentence in each case.

21. A. Do you know who it was?
    B. Beware of shopkeepers who engage in sharp practices.
    C. Elm trees have been planted among the trees in the grove.
    D. That is the same identical dress Jane wore last night.

22. A. I prefer the classical ballet to modern forms of the dance.
    B. Every sincere teacher is genuinely concerned with his pupils' progress.
    C. It is not easy to get use to commuting after years of living in the heart of the city.
    D. Reading, writing, speaking, and listening -- these are the main divisions of the subject called English.

23. A. If you would have called earlier, I would have been able to join you.
    B. The governor denied a pardon to the criminal since his record was extremely poor.
    C. On the tennis court, he was almost unbeatable.
    D. By leaving at noon, you can reach Chicago at three o'clock.

24. A. He couldn't bear to listen to the hypochondriac talking about his illnesses.
    B. Each year she went to the cemetary on Memorial Day.
    C. Some teachers, I believe, place too much emphasis on test results.
    D. Walking carefully over the grass, Jim avoided the new flower beds.

25. A. Almost all of our professional football players once played college football.
    B. Suddenly I remembered that I had forgotten the tickets.
    C. If I had thought of it, I would have called for you.
    D. I read in the newspaper where a close mayoralty race is predicted.

26. A. No sooner had he spoken to me, than I remembered his name.
    B. You are in this organization three years now and have not had a vacation.
    C. Not one of the children resembles his parents.
    D. The ship with all its passengers was lost.

27. A. His whisper was audible; even those in the rear clearly heard all he said.
    B. He felt compelled to eat what had been so lovingly prepared for him.
    C. Whether this book is their's or Mary's, it should be returned to the library.
    D. The sun set and the mosquitoes began to bite.

(Questions 21-30)

DIRECTIONS: In each of the following groups of sentences, one of the four sentences is faulty in capitalization, punctuation, grammar, spelling, sentence structure, diction, etc. Select the INCORRECT sentence in each case.

21. A. Do you know who it was?
    B. Beware of shopkeepers who engage in sharp practices.
    C. Elm trees have been planted among the trees of the grove.
    D. That is the same identical dress Jane wore last night.

22. A. I prefer the classical ballet to modern forms of the dance.
    B. Ivan since Leonore is seriously concerned with the pupils' progress.
    C. It is not easy to get use to commuting after years of living in the heart of the city.
    D. Reading, writing, speaking, and listening — these are the main divisions of the subject called English.

23. A. If you would have called earlier, I would have been able to help you.
    B. The government graded a raise to its employees since the record was extremely poor.
    C. On the tennis court, she was a smart opponent.
    D. By leaving at noon, you can reach Buffalo by three o'clock.

24. A. He couldn't bear to listen to the symphony or talking about his illnesses.
    B. Each year she went to the seashore or the mountains.
    C. Some typewriters like ours, since the much emphasis on time result.
    D. Neither careful cover the print, she avoided the new flower beds.

25. A. Almost all of our professional football players once played college football.
    B. Suddenly I remembered that I had forgotten the tickets.
    C. If I had thought so, I would have said so, you.
    D. I read in the newspaper where we close day, like mine is produced.

26. A. No sooner had we spoken to her, than I communicated his name.
    B. As he glared in amazement those years he had have not had a vacation.
    C. Not one of all the children remember his parents.
    D. The ship with all its passengers was lost.

27. A. His whispers audible, even those in the rear clearly heard all he said.
    B. He felt confident that the time had come for bringing pressure for him.
    C. Whether this book is theirs or hers, it should be returned to the library.
    D. The sun set and the mosquitoes began to bite.

Questions 21-35.

DIRECTIONS: In each of the following groups of sentences, one of the four sentences is faulty in capitalization, punctuation, grammar, spelling, sentence structure, diction, etc. Select the INCORRECT sentence in each case.

21. A. Do you know who it was?
    B. Beware of shopkeepers who engage in sharp practices.
    C. Elm trees have been planted among the trees in the grove.
    D. That is the same identical dress Jane wore last night.

22. A. I prefer the classical ballet to modern forms of the dance.
    B. Every sincere teacher is genuinely concerned with his pupils' progress.
    C. It is not easy to get use to commuting after years of living in the heart of the city.
    D. Reading, writing, speaking, and listening -- these are the main divisions of the subject called English.

23. A. If you would have called earlier, I would have been able to join you.
    B. The governor denied a pardon to the criminal since his record was extremely poor.
    C. On the tennis court, he was almost unbeatable.
    D. By leaving at noon, you can reach Chicago at three o'clock.

24. A. He couldn't bear to listen to the hypochondriac talking about his illnesses.
    B. Each year she went to the cemetary on Memorial Day.
    C. Some teachers, I believe, place too much emphasis on test results.
    D. Walking carefully over the grass, Jim avoided the new flower beds.

25. A. Almost all of our professional football players once played college football.
    B. Suddenly I remembered that I had forgotten the tickets.
    C. If I had thought of it, I would have called for you.
    D. I read in the newspaper where a close mayoralty race is predicted.

26. A. No sooner had he spoken to me, than I remembered his name.
    B. You are in this organization three years now and have not had a vacation.
    C. Not one of the children resembles his parents.
    D. The ship with all its passengers was lost.

27. A. His whisper was audible; even those in the rear clearly heard all he said.
    B. He felt compelled to eat what had been so lovingly prepared for him.
    C. Whether this book is their's or Mary's, it should be returned to the library.
    D. The sun set and the mosquitoes began to bite.

28. A. I think John, that you have missed the author's message.
    B. Whom were you referring to in the third paragraph?
    C. "Hurrah, we won!" shouted the excited boys.
    D. The consensus was that a woman would be the best teacher for the child.

29. A. Our secretary-treasurer has run away with the funds.
    B. Briefly, the functions of a military staff are to advise the commander, transit his instructions, and the supervision of the execution of his decisions.
    C. Novels contemporaneous with those of Scott are usually longer than modern novels.
    D. The publisher of this text states that it is far superior to that of his rival.

30. A. There are colloquial expressions which are common to all social classes.
    B. Being that you are here, we can proceed with the discussion.
    C. Mary bought the hat at once lest she change her mind.
    D. Since no one received permission to call the meeting, the plan was dropped.

31. A. I remember his exact words, "For next Thursday, finish reading 'The Ransom of Red Chief.'"
    B. Frequently the passers-by saw him at his work.
    C. Some children have a real flare for music.
    D. I spoke with John's mother about his work in my class.

32. A. Driving down the street, the car was overturned by the recklessness of the youngster at the wheel.
    B. The awkward waiter spilled soup all over my new dress.
    C. Yesterday afternoon, I lay down on the couch and fell asleep at once.
    D. We deplored their leaving early.

33. A. I had sooner die than betray my friends.
    B. Please take this book; it makes pleasant reading.
    C. The dog made off with a large piece of meat.
    D. The new employee didn't miss a day from work for five years, and which made him eligible for an award.

34. A. The argument that truth is relative and not absolute is invalid.
    B. Last winter we traveled through the Western part of Idaho and the Southern part of Illinois.
    C. A good many marital difficulties could be prevented from ending in divorce if there were more mutual understanding.
    D. "You may well get the job," said Bill, "but be sure you really want it."

35. A. It was Mr. Jones who gave my brother Tom and I our first job.
    B. An avid reader of science fiction, Gerald lived in a world of fantasy.
    C. We Americans "think big" only about economic problems; in matters political, we tend to be conservative.
    D. The prisoner was identified as a mental patient who the police said had escaped from an institution.

Questions 36-105.

DIRECTIONS: Every question or incomplete statement is followed by several suggested answers or completions. Select the one that BEST answers the question or completes the statement.

36. The practice of medicine plays a prominent role in each of the following novels EXCEPT
    A. SISTER CARRIE - Theodore Dreiser
    B. THE CITADEL - A.J. Cronin
    C. MAGNIFICENT OBSESSION - Lloyd C. Douglas
    D. ARROWSMITH - Sinclair Lewis

37. Goneril, Regan and Cordelia may be found in Shakespeare's
    A. THE TEMPEST   B. A WINTER'S TALE
    C. KING LEAR   D. OTHELLO

38. ".... and Thou
    Beside me singing in the Wilderness
    And Wilderness were Paradise enow."

    are the lines from the work of
    A. Gibran   B. Omar Khayyám   C. Spinoza   D. Thoreau

39. The setting for Rölvaag's GIANTS IN THE EARTH is the
    A. Russian steppes during the Revolution
    B. African plains of the Masai warriors
    C. Dakota Territory in the 19th century
    D. Norwegian fiords in the days of the pagan gods

40. All of the following are great Greek writers of tragedy EXCEPT
    A. Aristophanes   B. Aeschylus
    C. Euripides   D. Sophocles

41. The "theatre of the absurd" may be observed in the dramatic output of all EXCEPT
    A. Eugene Ionesco   B. Andre Malraux
    C. Jean Genet   D. Samuel Beckett

42. All of the following Negroes achieved fame as poets EXCEPT
    A. Paul Lawrence Dunbar   B. James Weldon Johnson
    C. Countee Cullen   D. James Baldwin

43. "The ice was here, the ice was there,
    The ice was all around;
    It cracked and growled, and roared and howled,
    Like noises in a swound;"

    are lines from
    A. THE RIME OF THE ANCIENT MARINER
    B. THE WASTELAND
    C. DOVER BEACH
    D. PARADISE LOST

44. Dickens created Uriah Heep, a symbol of cunning and hypocrisy, in his novel
    A. OUR MUTUAL FRIEND   B. DAVID COPPERFIELD
    C. DOMBEY AND SON   D. BLEAK HOUSE

45. MANCHILD IN THE PROMISED LAND was written by
    A. Claude Brown   B. LeRoi Jones
    C. Langston Hughes   D. Eldridge Cleaver

46. In the famous work by Jonathan Swift, Gulliver's travels take him to all these islands EXCEPT
    A. Lilliput   B. Brobdingnag
    C. Atlantis   D. Laputa

47. "The paths of glory lead but to the grave" was written by
    A. William Blake   B. Robert Burns
    C. Oliver Goldsmith   D. Thomas Gray

48. "Compensation," "Friendship" and "Self-Reliance" are essays written by
    A. Henry David Thoreau   B. Oliver Wendell Holmes
    C. Ralph Waldo Emerson   D. Henry Adams

49. The prize-winning play THE GREAT WHITE HOPE deals with
    A. the foibles of a well-known comedian
    B. the life of a black pugilist
    C. troubles in South Africa
    D. the trial of a captured war criminal

50. The short story THE MONKEY'S PAW involves
    A. three wishes   B. a costume ball
    C. a child's birthday party   D. a concert on the mall

51. "Yellow journalism" is MOST closely associated with
    A. Adolph Ochs   B. Horace Greeley
    C. Col. R.R.McCormick   D. William R. Hearst

52. The Supreme Court's decision in the 1954 case of "Brown vs. Board of Education" rested upon the words:
    A. "We hold these truths to be self-evident, that all men are created equal ......"
    B. "No state shall make or enforce any law which shall abridge the privileges or immunities of citizens of the United States"
    C. "No person ... shall be compelled in any criminal case to be a witness against himself...."
    D. "All persons born or naturalized in the United States ... are citizens of the United States ...."

53. Among the following, the EARLIEST third party in American history was the
    A. Know-Nothing party   B. Greenback party
    C. Progressive party   D. Populist party

54. The American tradition of freedom of the press traces its origin to the
    A. Zenger case
    B. Dartmouth College case
    C. Marbury vs. Madison case
    D. McCulloch vs. Maryland case

55. All of the following have written about cities and urban problems in the United States EXCEPT
    A. Lewis Mumford
    B. Lincoln Steffens
    C. Gifford Pinchot
    D. Jean Gottman

56. Our present unsatisfactory balance of payments position might be improved by an increase in
    A. imports into the United States
    B. United States loans and grants to foreign nations
    C. expenditures by United States tourists abroad
    D. exports from the United States

57. The Securities and Exchange Commission (SEC) is MOST concerned about
    A. the truthfulness of prospectuses
    B. setting margin requirements for listed stocks
    C. fixing the interest rates charged on brokers' loans
    D. enforcing the recent Supreme Court ban on conglomerates

58. "In their differing outlooks these two figures mark the beginnings of our two-party system" refers to
    A. John Adams and Aaron Burr
    B. Alexander Hamilton and Thomas Jefferson
    C. George Washington and Samuel Adams
    D. John Hancock and John Marshall

59. Each of the following is associated with a policy of General DeGaulle during his administration as President of France EXCEPT for
    A. making peace in Algeria
    B. strengthening the prestige and power of the legislature since its members were the most direct link to the will of the people
    C. keeping Great Britain out of the Common Market
    D. encourging France to leave NATO

60. A West African nation that has been seriously torn by civil war recently is
    A. Kenya   B. Rhodesia   C. Nigeria   D. Tanzania

61. Each of the following pairs a significant historical person with an idea he advocated EXCEPT
    A. Woodrow Wilson - the League of Nations as an instrument for keeping the peace
    B. Mohandas Gandhi - passive resistance to British laws
    C. George Marshall - economic aid to western European nations in order to contain communism
    D. Theodore Roosevelt - government encouragement of large trusts since big busines is the backbone of economic prosperity

54. The American tradition of freedom of the press traces its origin to the
    A. Zenger case   B. Dartmouth College case
    C. Marbury vs. Madison case   D. McCulloch vs. Maryland case

55. All of the following have written about cities and urban problems in the United States EXCEPT
    A. Lewis Mumford   B. Lincoln Steffens
    C. Gifford Pinchot   D. Jean Gottman

56. Our present unsatisfactory balance of payments position might be improved by an increase in
    A. imports into the United States
    B. United States loans and grants to foreign nations
    C. expenditures by United States tourists abroad
    D. exports from the United States

57. The Securities and Exchange Commission (SEC) in 1967 concerned about
    A. the truthfulness of prospectuses
    B. setting margin requirements for listed stocks
    C. fixing the interest rates charged on brokers' loans
    D. enforcing the recent Supreme Court ban on conglomerates

58. In their differing outlooks these two figures mark the beginnings of our two-party system. refers to:
    A. John Adams and Aaron Burr
    B. Alexander Hamilton and Thomas Jefferson
    C. George Washington and Samuel Adams
    D. John Hancock and John Marshall

59. Each of the following is associated with a policy of General DeGaulle during his administration as President of France EXCEPT
    A. making peace in Algeria.
    B. strengthening the prestige and power of the legislature since its members owe the most direct link to the will of the people.
    C. keeping Great Britain out of the Common Market
    D. encouraging France to leave NATO

60. A west African nation that has been seriously torn by civil war recently is
    A. Kenya   B. Rhodesia   C. Nigeria   D. Tanzania

61. Each of the following pairs a significant historical person with an idea he advocated EXCEPT
    A. Woodrow Wilson - the League of Nations as an instrument for keeping the peace
    B. Mohandas Gandhi - passive resistance to British laws
    C. George Marshall - economic aid to western European nations in order to contain communism
    D. Theodore Roosevelt - government encouragement of large trusts since big business is the backbone of economic prosperity

62. The writer who first warned the world of the dangers inherent in an uncontrolled population explosion was
    A. Thomas Malthus
    B. Charles Darwin
    C. Jean Lamarck
    D. Louis Pasteur

63. Each of the following items dealing with labor-management relations is correctly defined EXCEPT
    A. checkoff - collection of union dues by the employer
    B. mediation - the process by which a third party is brought into a labor-management dispute to make compromise proposals but which neither side is bound to accept
    C. lockout - a court order requiring the union leadership to call off an illegal strike
    D. union shop agreement - an agreement between labor-management that an employee does not have to be a member of the union before getting the job but requiring him to join the union within a specified time after being hired

64. THE WEALTH OF NATIONS by Adam Smith proposed the idea of
    A. laissez-faire
    B. utopian socialism
    C. cooperatives
    D. socialism

65. All of the following ancient civilizations developed in the Fertile Crescent EXCEPT
    A. Babylonia
    B. Assyria
    C. Phoenicia
    D. Greece

66. The growth of towns and trade in Europe resulted in
    A. more power for the nobles
    B. the rise of the bourgeoisie
    C. the Crusades
    D. a decline in the king's power

67. Each of the following is an accurate statement of a geographic fact EXCEPT:
    A. The Suez Canal connects the Mediterranean Sea and the Indian Ocean.
    B. The Strait of Gibraltar separates Spain from Morocco.
    C. The Adriatic Sea separates Italy from Tunisia.
    D. The Black Sea divides the USSR from Turkey.

68. Each of the following items correctly matches a member of President Nixon's Cabinet with the post he occupies EXCEPT
    A. John Mitchell - Attorney General
    B. William Rogers - Secretary of State
    C. Melvin Laird - Secretary of Defense
    D. Henry Fowler - Secretary of the Treasury

69. The President's veto of a bill passed by Congress is an example of
    A. the system of checks and balances
    B. the federal system of division of powers
    C. concurrent powers of the Presidency
    D. the implied powers derived from the elastic clause

62. The author who first warned the world of the dangers inherent in an uncontrolled population explosion was
A. Thomas Malthus   B. Charles Darwin
C. Jean Lamarck   D. Louis Pasteur

63. Each of the following terms dealing with labor-management relations is correctly defined EXCEPT
A. checkoff - collected union dues by the employer
B. mediation - the process by which a third party is brought into a labor-management dispute to make compromise proposals but which neither side is bound to accept
C. lockout - a labor offer requiring the union leadership to call off an illegal strike
D. union shop agreement - an agreement between labor-management that an employee does not have to be a member of the union before getting the job but requiring him to join the union within a specified time after being hired

64. THE SYSTEM OF NATIONS by Adam Smith proposed the idea of
A. laissez-faire   B. Utopian socialism
C. conservatism   D. Marxism

65. After the killing and out of Charles de Gaulle, the Fourth Government of the
A. Czechs   B. Israel
C. Hungarian   D. Greece

66. The growth of towns and trade in Europe resulted in
A. a greater need for the nobles
B. the rise of the bourgeoisie
C. the crusades
D. decline in Monarchial power

67. Each of the following terms correctly names one of Europe's chief canals
A. The Suez Canal connects the Mediterranean Sea and the Indian Ocean
B. The Strait of Gibraltar separates Spain from Morocco
C. The Kiel Canal separates Libya from Tunisia
D. The North Sea links Britain USSR from Norway

68. Each of the following items correctly matches a member of President Nixon's Cabinet with the post he currently held
A. John Mitchell - Attorney General
B. William Rogers - Secretary of State
C. Melvin Laird - Secretary of Defense
D. Henry Fowler - Secretary of the Treasury

69. The President's veto of a bill passed by Congress is an example
A. the system of checks and balances
B. the federal system of division of powers
C. concurrent powers of the judiciary
D. the implied powers derived from the elastic clause

70. The treaty of Nanking (1842) which ended the Opium War
    A. finally terminated the friction between the Chinese and Europeans
    B. ceded Hong Kong island to Great Britain
    C. was the first expression of the Open Door Policy
    D. included important cessions of land to Russia in Manchuria

71. Fossilized remains of plants and animals are MOST likely to be found in
    A. granite   B. lava   C. pitchblende   D. marble

72. Partial inability of certain cells to utilize glucose in the body is compensated for by the use of
    A. thyroxin   B. iodine   C. insulin   D. fluorine

73. Of the following, the pair of plants that belong to the same botanical family is
    A. clover and pea   B. radish and rose
    C. gladiolus and orchid   D. pine and ash

74. The star NEAREST the earth is
    A. the moon   B. Venus   C. the sun   D. North Star

75. An example of a weak acid is
    A. baking soda   B. vinegar
    C. lactose   D. alcohol

76. Adult frogs and toads feed MOSTLY on
    A. seeds and berries   B. water plants
    C. fish eggs   D. living insects

77. Cortisone is produced by the
    A. kidney   B. adrenal gland
    C. pancreas   D. liver

78. A device designed to convert patterns of sound vibrations into visible light patterns is the
    A. oscilloscope   B. stethoscope
    C. audiometer   D. radiometer

79. Tetanus bacteria can survive for a long time in the soil because of their ability to form
    A. antitoxins   B. root hairs
    C. cysts   D. spores

80. When a light ray strikes a mirror, the path taken by the ray forms angles with a perpendicular to the mirror that are known as angles of
    A. incidence and refraction
    B. deflection and refraction
    C. incidence and reflection
    D. deflection and deviation

70. The treaty of Nanking (1842) which ended the Opium War
    A. finally terminated the friction between the Chinese and Europeans
    B. ceded Hong Kong Island to Great Britain
    C. was the first expression of the Open Door Policy
    D. included important cessions of land to Russia in Manchuria

71. Fossilized remains of plants and animals are MOST likely to be found in
    A. granite   B. lava   C. pitchblende   D. marble

72. Partial inability of certain cells to utilize glucose in the body is compensated for by the use of
    A. thyroxin   B. iodine   C. insulin   D. fluorine

73. Of the following, the pair of plants that belong to the same botanical family is
    A. clover and pea   B. radish and rose
    C. gladiolus and orchid   D. pine and ash

74. The star NEAREST the earth is
    A. the moon   B. Venus   C. the sun   D. North Star

75. An example of a weak acid is
    A. baking soda   B. vinegar
    C. lactose   D. alcohol

76. Adult frogs and toads feed MOSTLY on
    A. seeds and berries   B. water plants
    C. fish eggs   D. living insects

77. Cortisone is produced by the
    A. kidney   B. adrenal gland
    C. pancreas   D. liver

78. A device designed to convert patterns of sound vibrations into visible light patterns is the
    A. oscilloscope   B. stethoscope
    C. audiometer   D. radiometer

79. Tetanus bacteria can survive for a long time in the soil because of their ability to form
    A. antitoxin   B. root hairs
    C. cysts   D. spores

80. When a light ray strikes a mirror, the path taken by the ray forms angles with a perpendicular to the mirror that are known as angles of
    A. incidence and refraction
    B. deflection and refraction
    C. incidence and reflection
    D. deflection and deviation

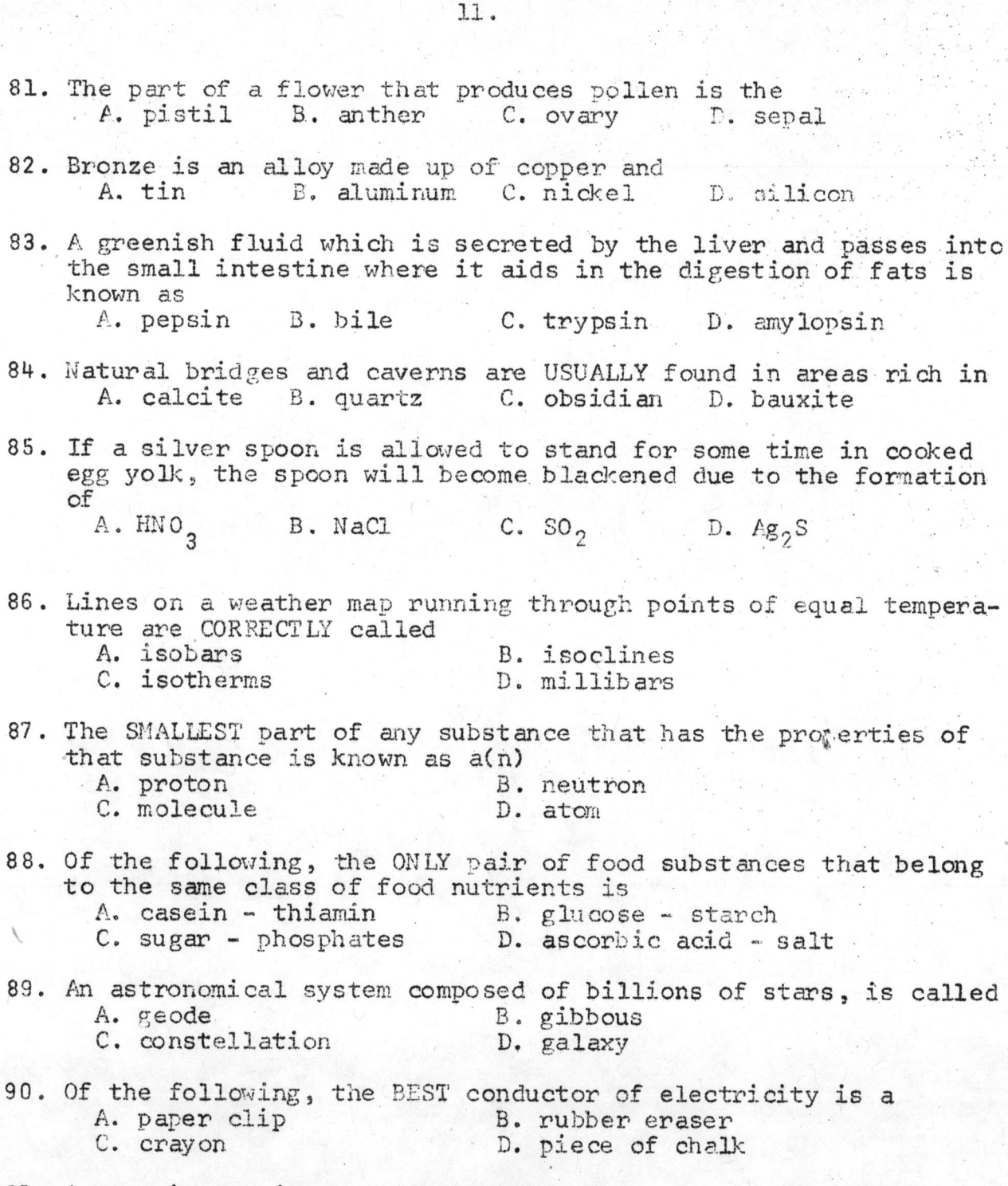

81. The part of a flower that produces pollen is the
    A. pistil   B. anther   C. ovary   D. sepal

82. Bronze is an alloy made up of copper and
    A. tin   B. aluminum   C. nickel   D. silicon

83. A greenish fluid which is secreted by the liver and passes into the small intestine where it aids in the digestion of fats is known as
    A. pepsin   B. bile   C. trypsin   D. amylopsin

84. Natural bridges and caverns are USUALLY found in areas rich in
    A. calcite   B. quartz   C. obsidian   D. bauxite

85. If a silver spoon is allowed to stand for some time in cooked egg yolk, the spoon will become blackened due to the formation of
    A. HNO_3 B. $NaCl$ C. SO_2 D. Ag_2S

86. Lines on a weather map running through points of equal temperature are CORRECTLY called
    A. isobars   B. isoclines
    C. isotherms   D. millibars

87. The SMALLEST part of any substance that has the properties of that substance is known as a(n)
    A. proton   B. neutron
    C. molecule   D. atom

88. Of the following, the ONLY pair of food substances that belong to the same class of food nutrients is
    A. casein - thiamin   B. glucose - starch
    C. sugar - phosphates   D. ascorbic acid - salt

89. An astronomical system composed of billions of stars, is called
    A. geode   B. gibbous
    C. constellation   D. galaxy

90. Of the following, the BEST conductor of electricity is a
    A. paper clip   B. rubber eraser
    C. crayon   D. piece of chalk

91. A song in a major key USUALLY ends on
    A. do   B. la   C. mi   D. sol

92. The twelve-tone scale is GENERALLY associated with
    A. Beethoven   B. Debussy
    C. Ravel   D. Schönberg

93. The key that is the relative minor to C major is
    A. C minor   B. A minor   C. E^b minor   D. G minor

94. Of the following musical forms, the one MOST closely allied to the round is the
    A. canon   B. sonata   C. fugue   D. rondo

95. Music based on ROMEO AND JULIET was written by all of the following EXCEPT
    A. Tschaikowsky   B. Bellini
    C. Brahms   D. Gounod

96. BILLY THE KID, RODEO and APPALACHIAN SPRING were composed by
    A. Aaron Copland   B. Charles Ives
    C. Edgar Varese   D. Lukas Foss

97. Of the following, the one who is NOT a famous singer is
    A. Beverly Sills   B. Myra Hess
    C. Christa Ludwig   D. Leontyne Price

98. The MOST imposing of all Roman circular temples is the
    A. Parthenon   B. Erechtheum
    C. Pantheon   D. Colosseum

99. The Guggenheim Museum on Fifth Avenue was designed by
    A. Frank Lloyd Wright B. Mies Van der Rohe
    C. Louis Sullivan   D. LeCorbusier

100. The city of Chartres in France is famous for its
    A. cathedral   B. frescoes
    C. tapestries   D. guild hall

101. The philosophy of pop art includes all the following EXCEPT
    A. banal subject matter   B. comment on modern art and life
    C. mystery and sentiment   D. ironical social message

102. Dali, the contemporary Spanish painter, is MOST known for his creative work in
    A. dadaistic painting   B. surrealistic painting
    C. expressionistic painting D. impressionistic painting

103. Primitive sculpture from the Congo and Ivory Coast GREATLY influenced the early work of
    A. Moore   B. Chagall   C. Picasso   D. Gauguin

104. Among the following painters, the one who is NOT of the Mexican mural tradition is
    A. Francisco Goya   B. Diego Rivera
    C. José Clemente Orozco D. Alfaro Siqueiros

105. A characteristic common to the painting of Gustave Courbet, Thomas Eakins and Winslow Homer is their
    A. concern with still life themes
    B. similarity of color palette
    C. preoccupation with surface rendering
    D. emphasis on realistic treatment

95. Music based on ROMEO AND JULIET was written by all of the fol-
lowing EXCEPT
A. Tschaikowsky   B. Berlioz
C. Brahms   D. Gounod

96. BILLY THE KID, RODEO and APPALACHIAN SPRING were composed by
A. Aaron Copland   B. Charles Ives
C. Edgar Varese   D. Lukas Foss

97. Of the following, the one who is NOT a famous singer is
A. Beverly Sills   B. Myra Hess
C. Christa Ludwig   D. Leontyne Price

98. The MOST important of all Roman circular temples is the
A. Parthenon   B. Erechtheum
C. Pantheon   D. Colosseum

99. The Guggenheim Museum on Fifth Avenue was designed by
A. Frank Lloyd Wright   B. Mies Van der Rohe
C. Louis Sullivan   D. LeCorbusier

100. The city of Chartres in France is famous for its
A. cathedral   B. frescos
C. tapestries   D. quail pail

101. The philosophy of pop art includes all the following EXCEPT
A. banal subject matter   B. comment on modern art and life
C. mystery and merriment   D. ironical social message

102. Dali, the contemporary Spanish painter, is MOST known for his
creative work in
A. dadaistic painting   B. surrealistic painting
C. expressionistic painting   D. impressionistic painting

103. Primitive sculpture from the Congo and Ivory Coast GREATLY
influenced the early work of
A. Moore   B. Chagall   C. Picasso   D. Sargent

104. Among the following painters, the one who is NOT of the Mexican
mural tradition is
A. Francisco Goya   B. Diego Rivera
C. José Clemente Orozco   D. Alfaro Siqueiros

105. A characteristic common to the paintings of Gustave Courbet,
Thomas Eakins and Winslow Homer is their
A. concern with still life themes
B. similarity of color palette
C. preoccupation with surface rendering
D. emphasis on realistic treatment

KEY (CORRECT ANSWERS)

1.	B	26.	B	51.	D	76.	D
2.	D	27.	C	52.	B	77.	B
3.	B	28.	A	53.	A	78.	A
4.	C	29.	B	54.	A	79.	D
5.	A	30.	B	55.	C	80.	C
6.	D	31.	C	56.	D	81.	B
7.	B	32.	A	57.	A	82.	A
8.	C	33.	D	58.	B	83.	B
9.	D	34.	C	59.	B	84.	A
10.	C	35.	A	60.	C	85.	D
11.	A	36.	A	61.	D	86.	C
12.	B	37.	C	62.	A	87.	C
13.	A	38.	B	63.	C	88.	B
14.	B	39.	C	64.	A	89.	D
15.	C	40.	A	65.	D	90.	A
16.	D	41.	B	66.	B	91.	A
17.	D	42.	D	67.	C	92.	D
18.	A	43.	A	68.	D	93.	A
19.	D	44.	B	69.	A	94.	A
20.	C	45.	A	70.	B	95.	C
21.	D	46.	C	71.	D	96.	A
22.	C	47.	D	72.	C	97.	B
23.	A	48.	C	73.	A	98.	C
24.	B	49.	B	74.	C	99.	A
25.	D	50.	A	75.	B	100.	A

101.	C
102.	B
103.	C
104.	A
105.	D

Questions 1-20.

DIRECTIONS: In each of the following groups, one sentence contains an underlined word which make the sentence INCORRECT. Select this sentence and indicate your choice on the answer sheet.

1. A. The silversmith inscribed his hallmark on the base of the silver vase.
   B. He was a man given to few words, garrulous by nature.
   C. She gesticulated wildly with her hands to emphasize her anger.
   D. The prizefighter dealt his opponent the quietus in the first round.

2. A. The children used colored glass to observe the ellipse of the sun.
   B. During the seance the participants observed the levitation of the body off the table.
   C. The savory dish was a culinary delight.
   D. The shrine of St. Catherine was declared sacrosanct by the church.

3. A. The river coursed through the country-side in sinuous curves.
   B. Joan of Arc was burned at the stake for her heretic beliefs.
   C. The mayor was so fair and impartial in his choice of appointees that he was praised for his nepotism.
   D. Cassandra's clairvoyance enabled her to foretell the future.

4. A. The judge permitted the attorney to submit arguments which were germane to the topic.
   B. Because she felt that the color blue enhanced her eyes, the actress had a penchant for blue clothes.
   C. After his arrest the thief was taken into court and arraigned
   D. At the apogee of their orbits the astronauts were closest to the earth.

5. A. They appointed a committee to consider the propriety of impeaching the governor.
   B. The driver found that he was unable to react quickly to prevent the accident.
   C. It is necessary for the scholar to take an occasional respite from his work if he is not to become fatigued.
   D. The prologue of the play followed the performance and summarized the action for the audience.

6. A. Noisome fumes are detrimental to health.
   B. Fettered to the wall, the prisoner could not escape.
   C. The poem was full of illusions to mythology.
   D. The lake shimmered with an opalescent sheen.

7. A. The customer's insults were utterly gratuitous, given without provocation.
   B. Politicians sometimes gerrymander their districts to gain more votes.
   C. His manner was so frank and surreptitious that he gained everybody's confidence.
   D. The necklace was filagree in design and lace-like in effect.

8. A. The appendix is a vestigial organ and therefore has important functions.
   B. The priest's vow of celibacy did not permit him to marry.
   C. The speaker went on and on boring the audience with his prolixity.
   D. John Kennedy held the public's attention by the charisma of his personality.

9. A. The manager's dour expression told us that his team had lost.
   B. The statesman was admired for his integrity and mendacity.
   C. Her vituperations would test the patience and tolerance of a saint.
   D. Advice becomes nugatory when given too freely or too often.

10. A. The accident was the result of culpable negligence on the part of the pilot.
    B. Mark Antony's incendiary speech stirred the Roman mob to riot and mutiny.
    C. Charles Dickens was skillful at delineating unusual personalities.
    D. An awed hush swept the audience as the maestro mounted the pediment.

11. A. The storekeeper's bellicose nature resulted in his being at peace with all.
    B. She needed no lipstick since her lips were a bright vermilion.
    C. The soil was exhausted and effete so that nothing could grow in it.
    D. The house on the hill commanded a broad vista of the woods below.

12. A. Gourmets enjoy vapid foods.
    B. The speaker's fulsome praise of the dictator sickened the audience.
    C. His flaccid muscles were the result of a sedentary life.
    D. The neglected wound became fetid.

13. A. Air pollution causes salubrious health conditions.
    B. To blame all ills of society on the schools alone is a simplistic argument.
    C. Iron is a ferrous metal.
    D. He had an irascible nature which caused him to get into many fights.

6. A. Noisome fumes are detrimental to health.
   B. Retreating to the wall, the prisoner could not escape.
   C. The poem was full of illusions to mythology.
   D. The lake shimmered with an eminescent sheen.

7. A. The customer's insults, were utterly gratuitous, given without provocation.
   B. Politicians sometimes gerrymander their districts to gain more votes.
   C. His manner was so frank and surreptitious that he gained everybody's confidence.
   D. The necklace was filigree in design and lace-like in effect.

8. A. The appendix is a vestigial organ and therefore has important functions.
   B. The priest's vow of celibacy did not permit him to marry.
   C. The speaker went on and on boring the audience with his prolixity.
   D. John Kennedy held the public's attention by the charisma of his personality.

9. A. The manager's dour expression told us that his team had lost.
   B. The statesman was admired for his integrity and mendacity.
   C. Her vituperations would rest the patience and reliance of a saint.
   D. Advice becomes purgatory when given too freely or too often.

10. A. The accident was the result of culpable negligence on the part of the pilot.
    B. Mark Antony's incendiary speech stirred the Roman mob to riot and mutiny.
    C. Charles Dick ns won skillful at delineating unusual personalities.
    D. An awed hush swept the audience as the maestro mounted the pediment.

11. A. The storekeeper's bellicose nature resulted in his being at peace with all.
    B. She needed no lipstick since her lips were a bright vermillion.
    C. The soil was exhausted and effete so that nothing could grow in it.
    D. The house on the hill commanded a broad vista of the woods below.

12. A. Gourmets enjoy viands foods.
    B. The speaker's fulsome praise of the dictator sickened the audience.
    C. His flaccid muscles were the result of a sedentary life.
    D. The neglected wound became fetid.

13. A. Air pollution causes salubrious nearby conditions.
    B. To blame all ills of society on the schools alone is a simplistic argument.
    C. Iron is a ferrous metal.
    D. He had an irascible nature which caused him to get into many fights.

14. A. The President spoke of the exploits of the astronauts in lauditory terms.
    B. The criminals were punished for their contemptible actions.
    C. The defending forces occupied an invulnerable position.
    D. The machinery was dissembled and prepared for storage.

15. A. The audience howled at the lecturer's risible remarks.
    B. The predilections of the fortune teller rarely proved to be correct.
    C. Pertinacious by nature, Michael refused to give up.
    D. The priest donned his sacerdotal garments.

16. A. The judge demurred at first but took action when he was pressed.
    B. The discursive document was a pleasure to read because of its succinctness and brevity.
    C. He deprecated the method used to resolve the problem.
    D. The dilatory tactics of the opposing army allowed them time to strengthen their position.

17. A. Jefferson's basic postulate was that all men are created equal
    B. The Mona Lisa's enigmatic smile has puzzled many.
    C. The speaker's manner was so ebullient that he put the audience to sleep.
    D. The lawyer was unable to effectuate the transfer of the property.

18. A. Robert poured drinks from a colorful ewer.
    B. The mainspring is an indispensable component of a watch.
    C. The parsimonious gentleman donated liberal sums to charity.
    D. The army was called upon to quell the insurrection.

19. A. Narcotics are often used to militate pain.
    B. The author used a caret to indicate an omitted word.
    C. During the earthquake, fissures appeared in the earth's crust.
    D. Deciduous trees shed their leaves in the fall.

20. A. The student understood the theory after its elucidation by the professor.
    B. She smoothed an emollient balm over the child's rough skin.
    C. The villain's sneering countenance gave him a malevolent air.
    D. His study habits were so systematic and desultory that he received an "A" in the course.

14. A. The President spoke of the exploits of the astronauts in laudatory terms.
    B. The criminals were punished for their contemptible actions.
    C. The defending forces occupied an invulnerable position.
    D. The machinery was disassembled and prepared for storage.

15. A. The audience howled at the lecturer's risible remarks.
    B. The predilections of the fortune teller rarely proved to be correct.
    C. Pertinacious by nature, Michael refused to give up.
    D. The priest donned his sacerdotal garments.

16. A. The judge demurred at first but took action when he was pressed.
    B. The discursive document was a pleasure to read because of its succinctness and brevity.
    C. He deprecated the method used to resolve the problem.
    D. The dilatory tactics of the opposing army allowed them time to strengthen their position.

17. A. Jefferson's basic postulate was that all men are created equal.
    B. The Mona Lisa's enigmatic smile has puzzled many.
    C. The speaker's manner was so ebullient that he put the audience to sleep.
    D. The lawyer was unable to effectuate the transfer of the property.

18. A. Robert poured drinks from a colorful ewer.
    B. The mainspring is an indispensable component of a watch.
    C. The parsimonious gentleman donated liberal sums to charity.
    D. The army was called upon to quell the insurrection.

19. A. Narcotics are often used to militate pain.
    B. The author used a caret to indicate an omitted word.
    C. During the earthquake, fissures appeared in the earth's crust.
    D. Deciduous trees shed their leaves in the fall.

20. A. The student understood the theory after the elucidation by the professor.
    B. She smoothed an emollient balm over the child's rough skin.
    C. The villain's sneering countenance gave him a malevolent air.
    D. His study habits were so systematic and desultory that he received an A+ in the course.

Questions 21-35.

DIRECTIONS: In each of the following groups of sentences, one of the four sentences is faulty in capitalization, punctuation, grammar, spelling, sentence structure, diction, etc. Select the INCORRECT sentence in each case.

21. A. If you listen to his sacrilegious talk, you will lose your perspective on moral questions.
    B. Did he say, "I am going now"?
    C. The class representatives are John, Bill, and I.
    D. After being wheeled into the operating room, a nurse placed a mask over my nose.

22. A. We girls insist on your giving them what is theirs and us what is ours.
    B. Do not infer from today's perfect attendance record that we have no truancy in this school.
    C. Instead of leaving this attendance book here, bring it to the principal's office.
    D. The reason for this request is that we must get ready for a monthly report to be submitted to the district superintendent.

23. A. Have you anything to say besides what we already know?
    B. She wore clothes that were better than the other girls.
    C. He reaffirmed on the same day his conviction that war is the greatest single sin of mankind.
    D. We hear dissent from a young man who, we firmly believe, is not about to pay compliments to our political leaders or to the local draft board.

24. A. Controversial matters involving the two classes were discussed nevertheless, most of the representatives remained calm.
    B. I don't know that I shall go.
    C. He has not and will not complete the work.
    D. We did not consider the matter further.

25. A. Whom did you say you met?
    B. We expected by the time the class convened to have received our grades on the mid-year tests.
    C. If he had lain quietly under the tree as he had been instructed to do, we would have found him.
    D. This search will be over soon; we shall find him somewheres.

26. A. We thought it wise to tell Mrs. Smith, she being the only early childhood teacher present.
    B. If one reads a great many articles in _Elementary English_, you will become familiar with the problems of the beginning teacher of reading.
    C. "It is you, who are a college graduate, who is mistaken about my theories on the education of the disadvantaged," said the professor.
    D. Acoustics is the scientific study of sound.

Questions 21-35.

DIRECTIONS: In each of the following groups of sentences, one of the four sentences is faulty in capitalization, punctuation, grammar, spelling, sentence structure, diction, etc. Select the INCORRECT sentence in each case.

21. A. If you listen to his acrrilegious talk, you will lose your perspective on moral questions.
    B. Did he say, "I am going now"?
    C. The class representatives are John, Bill, and I.
    D. After being wheeled into the operating room, a nurse placed a mask over my nose.

22. A. Is pride insist on your giving them what is theirs and us what is ours.
    B. Do not infer from today's perfect attendance record that we have no truancy in this school.
    C. Instead of leaving this attendance book here, bring it to the principal's office.
    D. The reason for this request is that we must get ready for a monthly report to be submitted to the district superintendent.

23. A. Have you anything to say besides what we already know?
    B. She wore clothes that were neater than the other girls.
    C. He testified on the same day his conviction that war is the greatest single sin of mankind.
    D. We hear dissent from a young man who, we firmly believe, is not about to pay compliments to our political leaders or to their dirty hands.

24. A. Controversial matters involving the two classes were discussed; nevertheless, most of the representatives remained calm.
    B. I don't know that I shall go.
    C. He has not and will not complete the work.
    D. We did not consider the matter further.

25. A. Whom did you say you met?
    B. We expected by the time the class convenes to have received our grades on the mid-year tests.
    C. If he had lain quietly under the tree as he had been instructed to do, we would have found him.
    D. This search will be over soon; we shall find him somewhere.

26. A. We thought it wise to tell Mrs. Smith, she being the only early childhood teacher present.
    B. If one reads a great many articles in Elementary English, you will become familiar with the problems of the beginning teacher of reading.
    C. "It is you, who are a college graduate, who is mistaken about my theories on the education of the disadvantaged," said the professor.
    D. Acoustics is the scientific study of sound.

27. A. If the principal will arrive before I leave, I shall describe to him what is permissible in the gym.
    B. Either the teacher or his students are responsible.
    C. The principal difficulty in judging these contests is that of finding competent critics.
    D. My brother-in-law is quicker than I.

28. A. Down the field came the students of South High School: members of the newly organized, somewhat incompetent band; drum majorettes in white, spangled skirts; and the team, muddy and wretched.
    B. The prettiest girl in the school sits beside me in the physics class.
    C. Ten miles is too far to walk.
    D. The main thing to see are the famous paintings.

29. A. The principal wants us all -- John, Helen, and me -- to run for office.
    B. "Fewer questions and less noise," shouted the president of the girls' club.
    C. A number of famous counselors are standing outside the courtroom waiting to find out about accomodations inside.
    D. The number of people who have queued up for tickets is eighty.

30. A. If I had been there, I would have taken care of the problem.
    B. This is a matter for settlement between you and me.
    C. He wanted to know was I going to accept the child in a first-grade class.
    D. I wish I were in Florida right now.

31. A. He believes in witchcraft, but he doubts that they ride on broomsticks.
    B. Between you and me, I believe this daguerreotype shows genuine artistry.
    C. Those who have had their surfeit of modern music often complain of the staccato effects.
    D. The principal argued for altering the curriculum; he wanted to eliminate vapidity and substitute vitality and relevance.

32. A. "Who knows" asked Bill, "how to find Jim's address"?
    B. The Indians are the true aborigines of our country.
    C. Civics is a course once taught in junior high school.
    D. Every precaution was taken to insure healthful conditions.

33. A. The visitors were all ready to enter the mysterious grotto.
    B. Being that you are interested in the outcome of the election, let us wait until the final tally has been made.
    C. Out of the mist loomed the first fragmentary vistas of tree-lined boulevards.
    D. The retreat of the enemy into caves and tunnels deceived the oncoming infantrymen.

27. A. If the principal will arrive before I leave, I shall describe to him what is permissible in the gym.
    B. Either the teacher or his students are responsible.
    C. The principal difficulty in judging these contests is that of finding competent critics.
    D. My brother-in-law is quicker than I.

28. A. Down the field came the students of South High School; members of the newly organized, somewhat incompetent band; drum majorettes in white, spangled skirts; and the team, muddy and drenched.
    B. The prettiest girl in the school sits beside me in the physics class.
    C. Ten miles is too far to walk.
    D. The main thing to see are the famous paintings.

29. A. The principal wants us all -- John, Helen, and me -- to run for office.
    B. "Fewer questions and less noise," shouted the president of the girls' club.
    C. A number of famous counselors are standing outside the courtroom waiting to find out about accomodations inside.
    D. The number of people who have queued up for tickets is mighty.

30. A. If I had been there, I would have taken care of the problem.
    B. This is a matter for settlement between you and me.
    C. He wanted to know was I going to spend the child in a first-grade class.
    D. I wish I were in Florida right now.

31. A. He believes in witchcraft, but he doubts that they ride on broomsticks.
    B. Between you and me, I believe this daguerreotype shows genuine artistry.
    C. Those who have had their surfeit of modern music often complain of the staccato effects.
    D. The principal argued for altering the curriculum; he wanted to eliminate vapidity and substitute vitality and relevance.

32. A. "Who knows," asked Bill, "how to find Jim's address?"
    B. The Indians are the true aborigines of our country.
    C. Civics is a course once taught in junior high school.
    D. Every precaution was taken to insure healthful conditions.

33. A. The visitors were all ready to enter the mysterious grotto.
    B. Seeing that you are interested in the outcome of the election, let us wait until the final tally has been made.
    C. Out of the mist loomed the first fragmentary vista of tree-lined boulevards.
    D. The retreat of the enemy into caves and tunnels deceived the oncoming infantrymen.

34. A. Walter, Jimmy, and myself went on a ten-mile hike.
    B. The millennium will have arrived when parents give appropriate responsibilities to us teen-agers.
    C. The crisis in Vietnam is one of the topics that have been discussed at our weekly forums.
    D. In contrast to his intellectual prowess were his slovenly appearance and his nervous demeanor.

35. A. Jack runs like Tom.
    B. Then we entered the hall where you could see a large crowd assembled.
    C. The legislator believed that his plan was practicable.
    D. Do you feel as bad as I do?

Questions 36-125.

DIRECTIONS: Each question or incomplete statement is followed by several suggested answers or completions. Select the one that BEST answers the question or completes the statement.

36. "In the spring a young man's fancy lightly turns to thoughts of love" is a quotation from the works of
    A. Henry Wadsworth Longfellow   B. Algernon Swinburne
    C. Alfred Lord Tennyson   D. Edna St.Vincent Millay

37. In the lines
    "The moan of doves in immemorial elms
    And murmuring of innumerable bees"
    can be found an example of
    A. simile   B. onomatopoeia
    C. synecdoche   D. hyperbole

38. All of the following essays were written by Charles Lamb EXCEPT
    A. DREAM CHILDREN   B. AN APOLOGY FOR IDLERS
    C. A DISSERTATION ON ROAST PIG   D. A CHARACTER OF THE LATE ELIA

39. The famous quotation "Hitch your wagon to a star" appears in an essay by
    A. Thomas Carlyle   B. John Galsworthy
    C. Ralph Waldo Emerson   D. Sir Francis Bacon

40. SHE STOOPS TO CONQUER, a play by Goldsmith, is about
    A. a governess who became a courtesan
    B. a wealthy widow who became a secretary
    C. an heiress who outwitted her sister to win a fortune
    D. a lady of quality who posed as a servant

41. The title of Hemingway's novel FOR WHOM THE BELL TOLLS is from the writings of
    A. Robert Browning   B. Thomas Gray
    C. William Cullen Bryant   D. John Donne

34. A. Walter, Jimmy, and myself went on a Teamster hike.
    B. The millennium will have arrived when parents give appropriate responsibilities to us teen-agers.
    C. The crisis in Vietnam is one of the topics that have been discussed at our weekly forums.
    D. In contrast to his intellectual prowess were his slovenly appearance and his nervous demeanor.

35. A. Jack runs like Tom.
    B. Then we entered the hall where you could see a large crowd assembled.
    C. The legislator believed that his plan was practicable.
    D. Do you feel as bad as I do?

Questions 36-123.

DIRECTIONS: Each question or incomplete statement is followed by several suggested answers or completions. Select the one that BEST answers the question or completes the statement.

36. "In the spring a young man's fancy lightly turns to thoughts of love" is a quotation from the works of
    A. Henry Wadsworth Longfellow   B. Algernon Swinburne
    C. Alfred Lord Tennyson   D. Edna St. Vincent Millay

37. In the lines
        "The moan of doves in immemorial Elms
        And murmuring of innumerable bees,"
    can be found an example of
    A. simile   B. onomatopoeia
    C. synecdoche   D. hyperbole

38. All of the following essays were written by Charles Lamb EXCEPT
    A. DREAM CHILDREN   B. AN APOLOGY FOR IDLERS
    C. A DISSERTATION ON ROAST PIG D. A CHARACTER OF THE LATE ELIA

39. The famous quotation "Hitch your wagon to a star" appears in an essay by
    A. Thomas Carlyle   B. John Galsworthy
    C. Ralph Waldo Emerson D. Sir Francis Bacon

40. SHE STOOPS TO CONQUER, a play by Goldsmith, is about
    A. a governess who became a countess
    B. a wealthy widow who became a secretary
    C. an heiress who outwitted her sister to win a fortune
    D. a lady of quality who posed as a servant

41. The title of Hemingway's novel FOR WHOM THE BELL TOLLS is from the writings of
    A. Robert Browning   B. Thomas Gray
    C. William Cullen Bryant D. John Donne

42. THANATOPSIS, a poem about death, was written by
    A. William C. Bryant when he was not yet twenty
    B. John Milton when Charles II was restored to power
    C. John Keats when he went to Italy for his health
    D. Rupert Brooke when he was a soldier in World War I

43. All of the following songs from Shakespeare are correctly associated with the plays in which they appear EXCEPT
    A. "Full fathom five thy father lies" - THE TEMPEST
    B. "Take, O take those lips away" - TAMING OF THE SHREW
    C. "Under the greenwood tree
       Who loves to lie with me" - AS YOU LIKE IT
    D. "Over hill, over dale,
       Thorough bush, thorough brier" - MIDSUMMER NIGHT'S DREAM

44. Dorothy Parker is noted MOST for her
    A. strong characterizations
    B. use of local color
    C. biting satire and caustic wit
    D. closely knit logical essays

45. THE STORY OF CIVILIZATION, a ten volume history hailed as a literary achievement, is the work of
    A. William Prescott   B. Vernon Parrington
    C. Will and Ariel Durant D. Van Wyck Brooks

46. An important modern novel which gives a striking picture of a single day's life is
    A. ULYSSES - James Joyce
    B. GONE WITH THE WIND - Margaret Mitchell
    C. APPOINTMENT IN SAMARRA - John O'Hara
    D. THE GREAT GATSBY - F. Scott Fitzgerald

47. Each of the following pairs is a correct association EXCEPT
    A. THE GREAT WHITE HOPE - the saga of a famous pugilist
    B. HADRIAN THE VII - the rise of an unorthodox pope
    C. THE PRICE - a kidnapper's demand for ransom
    D. THE MAN IN THE GLASS BOOTH - a Nazi war criminal on trial in Israel

48. A MAN FOR ALL SEASONS dealt with the life of
    A. Thomas a Becket   B. Sir Thomas Wyatt
    C. Sir Thomas Malory   D. Sir Thomas More

49. The aeronautical achievements of the modern era may easily remind one of the legendary figure of
    A. Daedalus   B. Sisyphus
    C. Midas   D. Orpheus

50. All the following poems and authors are correctly paired EXCEPT
    A. THE DAY IS DONE - Longfellow
    B. ANNABELLE LEE - Poe
    C. BARTER - Sara Teasdale
    D. RICHARD CORY - Robert Frost

42. THANATOPSIS, a poem about death, was written by
   A. William C. Bryant when he was not yet twenty
   B. John Milton when Charles II was restored to power
   C. John Keats when he went to Italy for his health
   D. Rupert Brooke when he was a soldier in World War I

43. All of the following songs from Shakespeare are correctly
    associated with the plays in which they appear EXCEPT
   A. "Full fathom five thy father lies," - THE TEMPEST
   B. "Take, O take those lips away," - TAMING OF THE SHREW
   C. "Under the greenwood tree
      Who loves to lie with me," - AS YOU LIKE IT
   D. "Over hill, over dale,
       Thorough bush, thorough brier," - MIDSUMMER NIGHT'S DREAM

44. Dorothy Parker is noted MOST for her
   A. strong characterizations
   B. use of local color
   C. biting satire and caustic wit
   D. closely knit lyrical essay

45. THE STORY OF CIVILIZATION, a ten volume history hailed as a lit-
    erary achievement, is the work of
   A. William Prescott   B. Vernon Parrington
   C. Will and Ariel Durant   D. Van Wyck Brooks

46. An important modern novel which gives a striking picture of a
    single Indian life is
   A. ULYSSES - James Joyce
   B. GONE WITH THE WIND - Margaret Mitchell
   C. APPOINTMENT IN SAMARRA - John O'Hara
   D. THE GOOD EARTH - Pearl S. Buck

47. Each of the following pairs is a correct association EXCEPT
   A. THE GREAT HUNGER - the saga of a famous pugilist
   B. HADRIAN THE VII - the rise of an unorthodox pope
   C. THE PRICE - a Kidnapper's demand for ransom
   D. THE MAN IN THE GLASS BOOTH - a Nazi war criminal on trial
                                    in Israel

48. A MAN FOR ALL SEASONS dealt with the life of
   A. Thomas a Becket   B. Sir Thomas Wyatt
   C. Sir Thomas Malory   D. Sir Thomas More

49. The sprit ritual achievements of the modern era are easily
    remindful one of the legendary figure of
   A. Aesculpus   B. Sisyphus
   C. Midas   D. Orpheus

50. All the following poems and authors are correctly paired EXCEPT
   A. THE DAY IS DONE - Longfellow
   B. ANNABELLE LEE - Poe
   C. BARTER - Sara Teasdale
   D. RICHARD CORY - Robert Frost

51. The HIGHEST latitude reading on a globe is
    A. 0 degrees
    B. 90 degrees
    C. 360 degrees
    D. 180 degrees

52. The French and Indian War was important MAINLY because it
    A. secured the expulsion of Spain from North America
    B. marked the final subjugation of the Canadian Indians by the French
    C. left only England and France as colonial powers in North America
    D. insured that the area west of the Appalachians would be settled by the English

53. The group that benefited MOST from the general economic policies pursued by the federal government during the latter part of the 19th century was the
    A. eastern factory workers
    B. western farmers
    C. southern plantation owners
    D. eastern industrialists

54. Each of the following statements is true EXCEPT:
    A. Of all the continents, Asia is the largest.
    B. The longest distance between two places on earth is a "great circle."
    C. The U.S.S.R. covers about 1/7 of the land area of the world.
    D. Asia has the largest percentage of the total population of the world.

55. Each of the following noted Americans is correctly matched with an idea he or she advocated EXCEPT:
    A. Patrick Henry - The American colonies should declare their independence from England.
    B. Lucretia Mott - Women ought to have the same political rights as men.
    C. Martin Luther King - The Negro should battle for civil rights without the use of violence.
    D. Alexander Hamilton - The American farmer is the backbone of the country.

56. In a course on Negro history, each of the following names will probably appear EXCEPT
    A. Marcus Garvey
    B. Toussaint L'Ouverture
    C. Charles W. Peale
    D. Nat Turner

57. Britain's international commercial policy during the 18th century is BEST described as
    A. mercantilism
    B. free trade
    C. feudalism
    D. laissez-faire capitalism

58. Each of the following statements regarding a country in Latin America is true EXCEPT:
    A. The Pampas is a region of broad, grassy plains covering the central part of Argentina.
    B. Most of Latin America is in the torrid zone.
    C. Mexico is a leading producer of silver.
    D. Brazil, like most of the Latin American countries, is a Spanish-speaking land.

51. The HIGHEST latitude reading on a globe is
    A. 0 degrees   B. 90 degrees
    C. 360 degrees   D. 180 degrees

52. The French and Indian War was important MAINLY because it
    A. assured the expulsion of Spain from North America
    B. marked the final subjugation of the Canadian Indians by the French
    C. left only England and France as colonial powers in North America
    D. insured that the area west of the Appalachians would be occupied by the English

53. The group that benefited MOST from the general economic policies pursued by the Federal government during the latter part of the 19th century was the
    A. eastern factory workers   B. western farmers
    C. southern plantation owners D. eastern industrialists

54. Each of the following statements is true EXCEPT:
    A. Of all the continents Asia is the largest.
    B. The longest distance between two places on earth is a half circle.
    C. The U.S.S.R. covers about 1/7 of the land area of the world.
    D. Asia has the largest percentage of the total population of the world.

55. Each of the following noted Americans is correctly matched with a phrase or thought EXCEPT:
    A. Patrick Henry - The American colonies should declare their independence from England.
    B. Thurgood Marshall - Women ought to have the same political rights as men.
    C. Martin Luther King - The Negro should strive for civil rights without the use of violence.
    D. Alexander Hamilton - The American farmer is the backbone of the country.

56. In a course on the to history each of the following names will probably appear EXCEPT:
    A. Marcus Garvey   B. Toussaint L'Ouverture
    C. Cinques   D. Nat Turner

57. Britain's international commercial relations during the 19th century is MOST described as
    A. mercantilism   B. free trade
    C. feudalism   D. laissez-faire capitalism

58. Each of the following statements regarding a country in Latin America is true EXCEPT:
    A. The Pampas is a region of broad, grassy plains covering the central part of Argentina.
    B. Most of Latin America is in the torrid zone.
    C. Mexico is a leading producer of silver.
    D. Brazil, like most of the Latin American countries, is a Spanish-speaking land.

59. The Industrial Revolution had its origin in
    A. England   B. Italy   C. France   D. Germany

60. A proposed amendment becomes a part of the Federal Constitution when it is ratified by
    A. Congress and signed by the President
    B. a majority vote of the people in each state
    C. the legislatures of three-fourths of the states
    D. a two-thirds vote of the House of Representatives

61. The Federal Reserve System was an improvement over the previous banking system in that the Federal Reserve System
    A. provided insurance for deposits up to $10,000
    B. provided for elasticity of currency
    C. guaranteed payment in gold in exchange for paper money
    D. made it possible for member banks to borrow money at lower rates of interest

62. The economist whose theory relates MOST directly to the "population explosion" is
    A. Adam Smith   B. Thorstein Veblen
    C. Thomas Malthus   D. John Keynes

63. All of the following are sub-disciplines of anthropology EXCEPT
    A. linguistics   B. cybernetics
    C. ethnology   D. archeology

64. The IMMEDIATE reason for the outbreak of World War II in Europe was the Nazi
    A. oppression of minorities   B. annexation of Austria
    C. invasion of Poland   D. absorption of Czechoslovakia

65. Each of the following is considered a satellite of the Soviet Union EXCEPT
    A. Yugoslavia   B. Hungary
    C. East Germany   D. Poland

66. The MAJOR objective of President John F. Kennedy's "Alliance for Progress" program was to
    A. contain the spread of Cuban revolutionary ideas
    B. strengthen the NATO Alliance
    C. render economic aid to many Latin American countries
    D. discourage the spread of dicatorship in South American countries

67. All of the following are members of President Nixon's cabinet EXCEPT
    A. David Kennedy   B. George Romney
    C. Robert Finch   D. George Ball

68. The meaning of a rise in the Consumer Price Index from 100 to 125 is that
    A. it takes $12.50 to buy what $10.000 bought in the base yea
    B. the dollar possesses 125% of its base year value
    C. $10.00 today buys what $12.50 bought in the base year
    D. the dollar's purchasing power has increased 25%

59. The Industrial Revolution had its origin in
    A. England   B. Italy   C. France   D. Germany

60. A proposed amendment becomes a part of the Federal Constitution when it is ratified by
    A. Congress and signed by the President
    B. a majority vote of the people in each state
    C. the legislatures of three-fourths of the states
    D. a two-thirds vote of the House of Representatives

61. The Federal Reserve System was an improvement over the previous banking system in that the Federal Reserve System
    A. provided insurance for deposits up to $10,000
    B. provided for elasticity of currency
    C. guaranteed payment in gold in exchange for paper money
    D. made it possible for member banks to borrow money at lower rates of interest

62. The economist whose theory relates MOST directly to the "population explosion" is
    A. Adam Smith   B. Thorstein Veblen
    C. Thomas Malthus   D. John Keynes

63. All of the following are sub-disciplines of anthropology EXCEPT
    A. linguistics   B. cybernetics
    C. ethnology   D. axiology

64. The IMMEDIATE reason for the outbreak of World War II in Europe was the Nazi
    A. appeasement of Chamberlain   B. annexation of Austria
    C. invasion of Poland   D. absorption of Czechoslovakia

65. Each of the following is considered a satellite of the Soviet Union EXCEPT
    A. Yugoslavia   B. Hungary
    C. East Germany   D. Poland

66. The MAJOR objective of President John F. Kennedy's "Alliance for Progress" program was to
    A. contain the spread of Cuban revolutionary ideas
    B. strengthen the NATO Alliance
    C. render economic aid to many Latin American countries
    D. discourage the spread of dictatorship in South American countries

67. All of the following are members of President Nixon's cabinet EXCEPT
    A. David Kennedy   B. George Romney
    C. Robert Finch   D. George Ball

68. The meaning of a rise in the Consumer Price Index from 100 to 125 is that
    A. it takes $12.50 to buy what $10.00 bought in the base year
    B. the dollar possesses 125% of its base year value
    C. $10.00 today buys what $12.50 bought in the base year
    D. the dollar's purchasing power has increased 25%

69. A piece of cork will submerge MOST when placed in
    A. olive oil   B. fresh water
    C. salt water   D. mercury

70. An electric motor turns because the electric current passing through its coils produces
    A. friction   B. radiation
    C. combustion   D. magnetism

71. The moon always presents the same face to the earth because of the nature of its
    A. orbital velocity   B. axis inclination
    C. rotation and revolution D. size and weight

72. An acid produced in the stomach which with the help of pepsin breaks down proteins into simpler substances is
    A. hydrochloric acid   B. sulphuric acid
    C. nitric acid   D. hydrobromic acid

73. An atmospheric pressure of 14.7 pounds per square inch will support a column of mercury of APPROXIMATELY
    A. 10 inches   B. 20 inches
    C. 30 inches   D. 40 inches

74. Snails are used in an ideal aquarium as
    A. oxygenators   B. scavengers
    C. coolants   D. fertilizers

75. At the lower end of mountain glaciers one is likely to find
    A. muskeg   B. moors
    C. mesas   D. moraines

76. A mineral used as an insulating material in electrical appliances is
    A. quartz   B. mica
    C. magnetite   D. lignite

77. The Mesabi Range is BEST known for its
    A. aluminum ore   B. copper ore
    C. nickel ore   D. iron ore

78. Limestone caves are formed by the action of ground water containing dissolved
    A. oxygen   B. chlorine
    C. carbon dioxide   D. iron oxide

79. A part of the inner ear that helps convert vibrations of sound waves into auditory nerve impulses is the
    A. cochlea   B. trachea
    C. ventricle   D. auricle

80. The part of the eye which focuses light rays is the
    A. iris   B. retina
    C. optic nerve   D. lens

69. A piece of cork will submerge MOST when placed in
    A. olive oil   B. fresh water
    C. salt water   D. mercury

70. An electric motor turns because the electric current passing
    through its coils produces
    A. friction   B. radiation
    C. combustion   D. magnetism

71. The moon always presents the same face to the earth because of its
    A. orbital velocity   B. axis inclination
    C. rotation and revolution   D. size and weight

72. An acid produced in the stomach which with the help of pepsin
    breaks down proteins into simpler substances is
    A. hydrochloric acid   B. (sulphuric) acid
    C. nitric acid   D. hydrochloric acid

73. An atmospheric pressure of 14.7 pounds per square inch will
    support a column of mercury of APPROXIMATELY
    A. 10 inches   B. 20 inches
    C. 70 inches   D. 80 inches

74. Snails are used in an home aquarium as
    A. thermometers   B. reservoirs
    C. coolants   D. scavengers

75. At the lower end of bones in placed one in its way to form
    A. muscles   B. roots
    C. bones   D. crutches

76. A mineral used as an insulating material in electrical appliances
    A. quartz   B. mica
    C. magnetite   D. ilmenite

77. The bauxit from it BPT known for the
    A. aluminum ore   B. copper ore
    C. nickel ore   D. iron ore

78. Limestone caves are formed by the action of ground water containing dissolved
    A. oxygen   B. silicates
    C. carbon dioxide   D. iron oxide

79. A part of the inner ear that helps convert vibrations of sound
    waves into auditory nerve impulses is the
    A. cochlea   B. trachea
    C. vestibule   D. eustachian

80. The part of the eye which focuses light rays is the
    A. iris   B. retina
    C. optic nerve   D. lens

81. The shrinkage and loss of cotyledons is visible during the growth and development of a
    A. bean plant
    B. bread mold
    C. tadpole
    D. chick embryo

82. The turning of a geranium leaf toward a source of light is an example of a type of behavior called
    A. commensalism
    B. translocation
    C. tropism
    D. simple reflex

83. A cloud formation that looks like a cauliflower or like heaps of fluffy cotton is known as a
    A. cirrus cloud
    B. cumulus cloud
    C. stratus cloud
    D. nimbus cloud

84. Of the following the one MOST likely to be hard water is
    A. ice water
    B. distilled water
    C. sea water
    D. rain water

85. Of the following plants, the one MOST likely to be found growing wild in the backyards of city houses is
    A. weeping beech
    B. tree of heaven
    C. burning bush
    D. Hercules' club

86. Of the following organisms, the ones MOST likely to destroy garden vegetables are
    A. earthworms
    B. bumblebees
    C. spiders
    D. slugs

87. Of the following great masters of music, the one who composed more than 200-piano pieces was
    A. Haydn
    B. Schubert
    C. Schumann
    D. Chopin

88. In PETER AND THE WOLF, the grandfather is portrayed by the
    A. horns   B. oboe   C. flute   D. bassoon

89. The sonata form is always used in
    A. overtures
    B. symphonies
    C. suites
    D. operas

90. The lyric for the well-known song DRINK TO ME ONLY WITH THINE EYES was written by
    A. Oliver Goldsmith
    B. Samuel Johnson
    C. Ben Jonson
    D. John Keats

91. Of the following operas, the one containing the MOST famous vocal quartet is
    A. FAUST
    B. RIGOLETTO
    C. LA TRAVIATA
    D. AIDA

92. Crescendo means to
    A. increase the tempo
    B. decrease the tempo
    C. increase the volume
    D. decrease the volume

81. The shrinkage and loss of cotyledons is visible during the growth and development of a
    A. bean plant   B. bread mold
    C. tadpole   D. chick embryo

82. The turning of a geranium leaf toward a source of light is an example of a type of behavior called
    A. compensation   B. translocation
    C. tropism   D. simple reflex

83. A cloud formation that looks like a cauliflower or like heaps of fluffy cotton is known as a
    A. cirrus cloud   B. cumulus cloud
    C. stratus cloud   D. nimbus cloud

84. Of the following, the one MOST likely to be hard water is
    A. ice water   B. distilled water
    C. sea water   D. rain water

85. Of the following plants, the one MOST likely to be found growing wild in the backyards of city houses is
    A. weeping beech   B. tree of heaven
    C. burning bush   D. Hercules' club

86. Of the following organisms, the ones MOST likely to destroy garden vegetables are
    A. earthworms   B. bumblebees
    C. spiders   D. slugs

87. Of the following great masters of music, the one who composed more than 200 piano pieces was
    A. Haydn   B. Schubert
    C. Schumann   D. Chopin

88. In PETER AND THE WOLF, the grandfather is portrayed by the
    A. horns   B. oboe   C. flute   D. bassoon

89. The sonata form is always used in
    A. overtures   B. symphonies
    C. suites   D. operas

90. The lyric for the well-known song DRINK TO ME ONLY WITH THINE EYES was written by
    A. Oliver Goldsmith   B. Samuel Johnson
    C. Ben Jonson   D. John Keats

91. Of the following operas, the one containing the MOST famous vocal quartet is
    A. FAUST   B. RIGOLETTO
    C. LA TRAVIATA   D. AIDA

92. Crescendo means to
    A. increase the tempo   B. decrease the tempo
    C. increase the volume   D. decrease the volume

93. The term "andante" indicates that the passage is to be sung or played
    A. in a lively manner		B. in a flowing manner
    C. with dramatic emphasis	D. mournfully

94. The CORRECT key signature for A major is
    A. 3 sharps		B. 1 sharp		C. 4 flats		D. 2 flats

95. Although Michelangelo was supremely gifted in several branches of art, he considered himself to be PRIMARILY a(n)
    A. painter			B. sculptor in marble
    C. architect		D. sculptor in bronze

96. All of the following architectural elements are Gothic in design, intent and style, EXCEPT the
    A. pointed arch		B. rose window
    C. flying buttress	D. dome

97. The painting titled GUERNICA in the Museum of Modern Art was painted by
    A. Velasquez		B. Goya
    C. Picasso			D. Magritte

98. All of the following have substantially influenced contemporary architectural design EXCEPT
    A. Walter Gropius		B. Frank Lloyd Wright
    C. Christopher Wren		D. Erro Saarinen

99. Depth in painting may be achieved by all the following EXCEPT
    A. overlapping of forms		B. interlocking forms
    C. mechanical perspective	D. decrease of size

100. An Impressionist painter whose allegiance to good draftsmanship is an apparent in his sculpture as it is in his paintings was
    A. Claude Monet		B. Edgar Degas
    C. Camille Pissarro	D. Edouard Manet

101. The art critic for the NEW YORK SUNDAY TIMES is
    A. John Canaday		B. Herbert Read
    C. Norman Cousins	D. Larry Rivers

102. "When I have selected the thing carefully, I paint it exactly as it appears," would BEST be attributed to
    A. Jackson Pollock		B. Marc Chagall
    C. Winslow Homer		D. Giacomo Bella

103. Of the following muscles, the one that is located in the lower extremity is the
    A. sartorious		B. pectoralis major
    C. biceps			D. trapezius

104. With reference to fractures of the bones a "simple fracture" means that
    A. the break is not serious
    B. medical attention is not necessary
    C. one of the smaller bones is involved
    D. the skin is unbroken

12.

95. The term "andante" indicates that the passage is to be sung or played
   A. in a lively manner.   B. in a flowing manner
   C. with dramatic emphasis. D. mournfully.

96. The CORRECT key signature for A major is
   A. 3 sharps.   B. 1 sharp.   C. 4 flats.   D. 2 flats

95. Although Michelangelo was supremely gifted in several branches of art, he considered himself to be PRIMARILY a(n)
   A. painter.   B. sculptor in marble
   C. architect.   D. sculptor in bronze.

96. All of the following architectural elements are Gothic in design, intent and style, EXCEPT the
   A. pointed arch.   B. rose window
   C. flying buttress.   D. dome.

97. The painting titled GUERNICA in the Museum of Modern Art was painted by
   A. Velasquez   B. Goya
   C. Picasso   D. Magritte

98. All of the following have substantially influenced contemporary architectural design EXCEPT
   A. Walter Gropius.   B. Frank Lloyd Wright
   C. Christopher Wren.   D. Eero Saarinen.

99. Depth in painting may be achieved by all the following EXCEPT
   A. overlapping of forms.   B. interlocking forms
   C. mechanical perspective. D. decrease of size.

100. An Impressionist painter whose allegiance to good craftsmanship is as apparent in his sculpture as it is in his paintings was
   A. Claude Monet.   B. Edgar Degas
   C. Camille Pissarro.   D. Edouard Manet

101. The art critic for the NEW YORK SUNDAY TIMES is
   A. John Canaday.   B. Herbert Read
   C. Norman Cousins.   D. Larry Rivers

102. "When I have selected the thing carefully, I paint it exactly as it appears," would BEST be attributed to
   A. Jackson Pollock.   B. Yigro Tamayo
   C. Winslow Homer.   D. Glackens.

103. Of the following muscles, the one that is located in the lower extremity is the
   A. sartorious.   B. pectoralis major
   C. biceps.   D. trapezius

104. With reference to fractures of the bones a simple fracture means that
   A. the break is not serious
   B. medical attention is not necessary
   C. one of the smaller bones is involved
   D. the skin is unbroken

105. All of the following athletes are correctly paired with their sport EXCEPT
    A. Bob Gibson - baseball
    B. O.J. Simpson - golf
    C. Jean-Claude Killy - skiing
    D. Arthur Ashe - tennis

106. Of the following sports, the one in which a participant would engage in a "giant slalom" is
    A. surfing   B. sprinting
    C. skiing   D. sailing

105. All of the following athletes are incorrectly paired with their sport EXCEPT:
   A. Bob Gibson - baseball
   B. O.J. Simpson - golf
   C. Jean-Claude Killy - skiing
   D. Arthur Ashe - tennis

106. Of the following sports, the one in which a participant would engage in a "giant slalom" is
   A. surfing   B. sprinting
   C. skiing   D. sailing

KEY (CORRECT ANSWERS)

1.	B	26.	B	51.	B	76.	B
2.	A	27.	A	52.	D	77.	D
3.	C	28.	D	53.	D	78.	C
4.	D	29.	C	54.	B	79.	A
5.	D	30.	C	55.	D	80.	D
6.	C	31.	A	56.	C	81.	A
7.	C	32.	A	57.	A	82.	C
8.	A	33.	B	58.	D	83.	B
9.	B	34.	A	59.	A	84.	C
10.	D	35.	B	60.	C	85.	B
11.	A	36.	C	61.	B	86.	D
12.	A	37.	B	62.	C	87.	D
13.	A	38.	B	63.	B	88.	D
14.	D	39.	C	64.	C	89.	B
15.	B	40.	D	65.	A	90.	C
16.	B	41.	D	66.	C	91.	B
17.	C	42.	A	67.	D	92.	C
18.	C	43.	B	68.	A	93.	B
19.	A	44.	C	69.	A	94.	A
20.	D	45.	C	70.	D	95.	B
21.	D	46.	A	71.	B	96.	D
22.	C	47.	C	72.	A	97.	C
23.	B	48.	D	73.	C	98.	C
24.	C	49.	A	74.	B	99.	B
25.	D	50.	D	75.	D	100.	B

101.	A
102.	C
103.	A
104.	D
105.	B
106.	C

KEY (CORRECT ANSWERS)

1. B		26. B		51. C		76. D	
2. A		27. A		52. C		77. D	
3. C		28. D		53. D		78. C	
4. C		29. D		54. B		79. A	
5. D		30. C		55. D		80. D	
6. C		31. A		56. C		81. K	
7. C		32. A		57. A		82. C	
8. A		33. B		58. D		83. B	
9. C		34. A		59. A		84. C	
10. D		35. B		60. C		85. B	
11. A		36. C		61. B		86. D	
12. A		37. C		62. D		87. D	
13. A		38. B		63. B		88. D	
14. C		39. C		64. C		89. C	
15. B		40. D		65. A		90. C	
16. D		41. C		66. C		91. D	
17. C		42. C		67. D		92. C	
18. C		43. B		68. A		93. B	
19. A		44. C		69. A		94. A	
20. B		45. C		70. T		95. B	
21. D		46. A		71. D		96. D	
22. D		47. C		72. A		97. C	
23. B		48. A		73. C		98. C	
24. C		49. A		74. B		99. D	
25. D		50. D		75. D		100. B	

101. A
102. C
103. A
104. C
105. B
106. C

BASIC PRINCIPLES AND PRACTICES IN EDUCATION
THE NEW PROGRAM OF EDUCATION

I. PHILOSOPHY AND OBJECTIVES

A. PHILOSOPHY
 1. An analysis of the aims and purposes of education
 2. An appraisal of current educational practices
 3. A statement of the "ideal" to be attained
 4. A justification of the means to be employed
B. CONCEPTS OF EDUCATION
 1. Education as knowledge
    a. Emphasis on factual learning
    b. Transmitting the past heritage
    c. Excessive use of texts
 2. Education as discipline
    a. Training the memory, imagination, etc.
    b. Emphasis on rote memory, drill, frequent tests, etc.
    c. Reliance on theory of transfer of training
 3. Education as growth
    a. Developing latent capacities and realization of child's potentialities
    b. Experiential and functional learning
    c. Emphasis on attitudes, appreciations, and interests
    d. Child-centered curriculum
    e. Stress on social relationships and democratic living procedures
C. OBJECTIVES
 1. Character - ethical living in a society promoting the common welfare
 2. American Heritage - faith in American democracy and respect for dignity and worth of the individual regardless of race, religion, nationality or socio-economic status
 3. Health - sound body and wholesome mental and emotional development
 4. Exploration - discovery and development of individual aptitudes
 5. Thinking - develop ability to reason critically, using facts and principles
 6. Knowledges and skills - command of common integrating knowledges and skills
 7. Appreciation and expression - appreciation and enjoyment of beauty and development of powers of creative expression
 8. Social relationships - develop desirable social relationships at home, in school, in the community
 9. Economic relationships - appreciation of economic processes and of contributions of all who serve in the world of work

MNEMONIC DEVICE FOR REMEMBERING THESE OBJECTIVES
T hinking   K nowledges and skills
E xploration   A ppreciation
A merican heritage   S ocial relationships
C haracter   E conomic relationships
H ealth

D. METHOD OF ACHIEVING THESE OBJECTIVES
1. Former emphasis on content with limited worthwhile, real experiences. Present stress on experiences with content used as a means to an end rather than as an end in itself.
2. This calls for a reorganization of our courses of study. Organization will now be in related areas rather than in separate isolated syllabi.
   These areas include:
   a. Pupil participation - to include planning, routines, and housekeeping, responsibilities, exploring school and community activities.
   b. Health - to include health instruction and guidance, safety education, rest, recreation, emotional adjustment, nutrition.
   c. Art - to include experimenting, use of various media as means of expression, practical applications in home, school, and community.
   d. Music - vocal, instrumental, rhythmic for enjoyment, expression, and understanding.
   e. Language Arts - reading, literature, composition, spelling, penmanship, speech, listening, dramatization.
   f. Social Studies - history, geography, civics, character, family relationships, consumer problems, intercultural education, citizenship and concepts of democracy.
   g. Science - nature study, weather, plants and soil, animals, earth and sky, food and water, tools and instruments, simple machines and electrical devices, flightcraft.
   h. Arithmetic - size, space, distance, time, weight, concepts, computations, problem solving.

   MNEMONIC DEVICE FOR THESE AREAS
   H ealth   L anguage Arts
   A rithmetic   A rt
   S ocial Studies   M usic
                      P upil participation
                      S cience

E. ORGANISMIC PSYCHOLOGY *(our current program is based chiefly on these principles)*
   1. The principle of continuous growth - This emphasizes the flexible, experimental, emergent nature of the individual and of society; it stresses the continuity of experience. (Aspects: continuous progress plan; constant curriculum revision.)
   2. The principle of experience as the method of learning - This emphasizes learning through functional, real experiences as opposed to memorization, drill, dictated assignments, etc. (Aspects: excursions; planning; research; reporting.)
   3. The principal of integration - This emphasizes the wholeness and unity of individuals and of society. It stresses the interaction between the learner and the learning situation and demands maximum life-likeness in learning situations. (Aspects: units; use of community resources; large areas of instruction; larger time-blocks

F. UNDERLYING TENETS OF THE PROGRAM
   1. Education of the whole child - social, civic, intellectual, ethical vocational
   2. Learning through real, functional experiences (activity vs. passivity)

3. The "intangibles" as an important end of education (interests, attitudes, character, etc.)
4. The concept of the child-centered school as opposed to the subject-centered school
5. The inclusion of the nine objectives of education as a part of educational planning at every step

G. WHAT DOES THE NEW PROGRAM MEAN?
 1. These things are basic:
    a. Socialization of procedures
    b. Integration of personality (before integration of subject matter)
    c. Increased pupil-teacher participation in planning and evaluating the educative process
    d. Group procedures
    e. A program to meet the individual's time-table of growth as well as a general development time-table
    f. First-hand experiencing as a "must" in education
    g. A mental hygiene viewpoint for the teacher
    h. Closer relationship between school-life and life in the world outside
    i. An acceptance of the view that concomitant learnings can sometimes be more important than the original learnings to be taught
 2. It is NOT merely:
    a. Unit development
    b. Correlation of subject matter
    c. Working through committees
    d. Provision for research activities
    e. Emphasis on reporting and discussion
    f. Planning for a culmination
    g. Keeping diaries and logs

H. ADVANTAGES AND DISADVANTAGES
 1. Proponents of the New Program maintain that this program:
    a. Provides a flexible content
    b. Encourages individual aptitudes
    c. Permits much practice in social behavior
    d. Encourages independent learning
    e. Encourages creative expression
    f. Provides a vitalized curriculum
    g. Permits greater integration of subject matter
    h. Provides for leisure-time activities
    i. Provides a success program for each child
    j. Makes greater provision for diagnosis, guidance, and individual remedial treatment
    k. Contributes abundantly towards the development of good character
 2. Opponents of the New Program maintain that:
    a. There is no gradation of the difficulties of different units of work
    b. It is not true to life (since life is not a series of activities)
    c. Too much reliance is placed on incidental learning
    d. There is no provision for participation by every child
    e. Teachers have not been trained sufficiently
    f. Equipment is underemphasized
    g. The interests of children are not sufficient as a guide for subject matter

h. The superficial aspects are overemphasized
i. Many important "learnings" are omitted
j. No provision is made for duplication in the case of pupils who are transferred or admitted

I. TRADITIONAL VS. PROGRESSIVE EDUCATION

TRADITIONAL   *PROGRESSIVE*

1. PHILOSOPHY

TRADITIONAL	PROGRESSIVE
a. School is a preparation for life	a. School is "life itself"
b. Emphasis on social heritage	b. Development of whole personality-knowledge, attitudes, morals, health
c. Adjust pipil to society that arises	c. School aims to improve society

2. CURRICULUM

TRADITIONAL	PROGRESSIVE
a. Factual curriculum laid out in advance for all	a. Subject matter - vital, purposeful, integrated, flexible, follows child's interests
b. Subjects clearly separated and isolated	b. Long units, integration and correlation of subject matter
c. Emphasis on memorization	c. Learning through experiences
d. Slavish use of text books	d. Use of a variety of reference and source materials

3. ROLE OF TEACHER

TRADITIONAL	PROGRESSIVE
a. Dominant factor in the learning process	a. Teacher is a guide and helper
b. Pupil passivity	b. Socialization and maximum pupil participation

4. METHODS

TRADITIONAL	PROGRESSIVE
a. Stressed mastery of subject matter	a. Adjustment of curriculum to needs, interests, and capacities of each child
b. Isolated drills. Extrinsic	b. Functional learning. Individualized drill at the point of error. Intrinsic
c. Rigid, formal discipline	c. A hum of activity. Self-discipline. Social adjustment
d. Inside of schoolroom	d. Excursions and field trips

5. SUPERVISION

TRADITIONAL	PROGRESSIVE
a. Dictatorial and inflexible	a. Democratic, scientific, creative
b. Teachers rated according to ability in achieving grade standards (standardized tests)	b. Teachers judged on basis of their ability to promote desirable attitudes - interests, appreciations, etc. (attitude tests and case histories)

J. GENERAL PRINCIPLES IN ANY MODERN PHILOSOPHY OF ELEMENTARY EDUCATION
1. Education must be democratic, universal, and compulsory
2. There must be a unifying philosophy for the school system as a whole
3. This philosophy must be essentially a social philosophy; the school must adjust children to a changing social order
4. The curriculum must be flexible and must be subject to frequent (continuous) revision
5. There must be flexibility in classroom procedures
6. Adequate equipment must be provided
7. Adequate provision must be made for the mentally and physically handicapped

II. THE CURRICULUM

A. DEFINITIONS
   1. The *CURRICULUM* consists of all the experiences, including all the subject matter and skills, which are utilized and interpreted by the school to further the aims of education. These experiences result from interaction between persons, influences, and material facilities. Some of the factors which effect the curriculum are:
      a. The political, economic, and social structure of the surrounding society
      b. The public opinion toward education
      c. The aims and philosophies of those operating the educational system
      d. The decisions concerning methods and materials, teacher selection, sarlaries, and physical plant
      e. The course of study, or, more properly, the documents made available to the teachers
   2. Early *COURSES OF STUDY* usually consisted only of a subject-matter outline; later ones included also some suggested learning activities, teaching procedures, diagnostic devices, and evaluation techniques. The emphasis, in all instances, was on "prescribed" subject matter to be covered, and some courses of study even specified the number of minutes per day to be devoted to each of the segments and the specific fact questions to be used.
   3. Modern *GUIDES* for teachers are not usually called courses of study. They suggest a wealth of materials and experiences; far from minimizing subject matter, they suggest more of it better adapted for use with varying levels of abilities and interests. They include bulletins on:
      a. the teaching of various subjects
      b. the organization of experience units with subject lines disregarded
      c. the characteristics of children
      d. varied learning experiences
      e. teaching procedures
      f. ways of using different types and amounts of subject matter
      g. sources of instructional aids
      h. evaluational techniques
      i. bibliographies, etc.

B. GENERAL CONSIDERATIONS
   1. A curriculum develops in answer to the needs of a group of learners and to the demands of a given society.
   2. A curriculum is made by a teacher and her pupils as they work together in the school.
   3. The development of a specific curriculum is a cooperative activity in which many persons participate (superintendents, principals, teachers, subject-matter specialists, consultants, school psychologists, pupils, parents, social agencies, advisory commissions, etc.)
   4. A program of curriculum improvement involves a study of:
      a. the political, economic, and social structure of the surrounding society
      b. public opinion toward education
      c. advice or information for the public
      d. the aims and philosophy of current educational practice

   e. the abilities, needs, purposes and individual differences among the learners
   f. the origin and nature of subject matter
   g. the development of present curriculums
   h. the nature of modern outcomes of learning
   i. the many new techniques of evaluation
  5. A program of curriculum improvement is far broader than the writing of a course of study or series of teachers' guides; it is concerned with the improvement of living and learning conditions in the school and in the community of which it is a part.
  6. A program of curriculum improvement should result in changes of attitudes, appreciations, and skills on the part of the participants and in important changes in the learning situation.
C. CONDITIONS THAT COMPEL CURRICULAR CHANGES
  1. Technological developments - In a society where most people work for someone else, it is important that the curriculum emphasize the attitudes and skills of cooperation.
  2. International problems - The curriculum must emphasize international understanding as well as the defense of America and other freedom-loving nations.
  3. Social change - The curriculum must prepare children for living in a complex and changing world, and must emphasize moral responsibility for one's acts both as an individual as well as a member of a group.
  4. Educational progress - The increase of available materials of instruction and the expanding role of the teacher call for a redistribution of teachers' time and energies in terms of a new set of values.
D. CHANGES THAT RESULT FROM CURRICULUM IMPROVEMENT
  1. In the professional staff-cooperative planning; working together on educational problems; experimentation with promising procedures; study of human growth and development.
  2. In the teaching-learning situation - improvement in the school plant, equipment, and supplies; use of community resources; available community services; opportunities for children to participate in community life.
  3. In improved pupil behavior - ability to define and solve meaningful problems: development of new interest; self-evaluation; skill in communication; skill in human relations; initiative; creativeness.
  4. In community relationships - participation by lay citizens; public support; public relations.
  5. In school organization - plan of organization; staff selection procedures; school size; class size; daily schedules; district services; faculty conferences.
  6. In instructional materials - cooperative production of instructional materials; more effective use of commercial materials; better selection of teaching aids; establishment of a "materials center"; development of a professional library.
  7. In ways of working together - teacher-pupil planning; group dynamics; sociometric techniques; intergroup education.
E. MAIN PROBLEMS IN CURRICULUM DEVELOPMENT
  1. The determination of educational directions
  2. The selection of experiences comprising the educational program
  3. The selection of a pattern of curriculum organization

4. The determination of principles and procedures by which the curriculum can be evaluated and changed

F. FACTORS AFFECTING CURRICULUM DEVELOPMENT
1. The existing political, economic, and social structure
2. Pressure exerted by minority groups or vested interests
3. Legislation
4. Tradition
5. Influence of logically organized subject matter and compartmentalization
6. Textbooks

G. CONSIDERATIONS FOR CURRICULUM PROGRAMS
1. The improvement program is to be developed with the aid of supervisors, teachers, pupils, parents, and community.
2. The curriculum should be readily adaptable to individual differences, needs, and interests and to the special needs of groups, schools and communities.
3. There should be provision for articulation between and among the various divisions and levels of the school system.
4. There must be provision for continuous experimentation and research.
5. There must be flexibility and allowance for interpretation and change to meet new situations and conditions.
6. There must be provision for evaluation of principles, practices, and outcomes, as well as for appraisal of the curriculum improvement program itself.
7. The curriculum must provide conditions, situations, and activities favorable to the continuous growth and progress of each individual.
8. Curriculum policies and practices should encourage friendly understanding and democratic relations among supervisors, teachers, pupils and parents.
9. The success of a curriculum is dependent on competent leadership. (Supervision interprets and implements the curriculum and seeks to improve teaching and learning; teachers' attitudes and understandings determine the effectiveness of the curriculum; community aims, purposes, and resources exert an important influence on the curriculum; pupils help in developing a wholesome pattern of democratic living in which the curriculum operates most effectively.)

H. QUESTIONS RELATED TO CURRICULUM DEVELOPMENT
1. Why is the traditional curriculum, used with seeming success for years, now under such criticism, analysis, and change?
2. Is the curriculum an instrument of social progress?
3. Should the aims of education and the content of the curriculum be determined with some definiteness in advance of actual teaching-learning situations?
4. Is all, none, or a given part of the curriculum to be required of all learners - regardless of origin, present status, and very probable destiny?
5. How shall the curriculum be organized - scope and sequence determined?
6. How shall the curriculum content be selected?
7. What are the desired outcomes of learning experiences?
8. How much of the curriculum can be formulated by the pupils?
9. What stand shall the curriculum take on "indoctrination?"

10. What procedures should be used in reconstructing the curriculum?
11. What are the criteria for evaluating a curriculum?

III. GROUPING AND COMMITTEE WORK

A. ORGANIZING GROUPS FOR INSTRUCTION
   1. Know the children before you group
      a. General level of achievement (standardized tests)
      b. Individual problems in the area (everyday performance)
      c. Capacity to achieve (expectancy)
      d. Personal and social adjustment (sociogram)
   2. Develop a "readiness" for grouping
      a. Teach the techniques that will be the basis for independent activity later
      b. Be familiar with the types of exercises to be used for group work later; anticipate some of the skills which will be required
      c. Develop work-skills (choosing something, sharing materials, working independently, etc.)
   3. Launch the best group first
      a. The first group will be those children most advanced intellectually and socially
      b. The remainder of the class learns to work independently as the teacher works with the first group
      c. As both these groups learn to work simultaneously, the teacher notes the point at which further subdivision becomes necessary (for example, the slower group may be broken down into a normal and slow group)
   4. Group standards should be set cooperatively by the teacher and class
   5. Some abilities to aim for:
      a. Working alone
      b. Working quietly
      c. Completing a job
      d. Moving to the next job when the present one is completed
      e. Finding and correcting one's errors
      f. Evaluating one's own work
   6. Arrangement of pupils
      a. Reduce to a minimum the interference of one group with another (through location of groups in the room, allocation of blackboard space, etc.)
      b. Have a group's materials placed near to where that group works
B. CRITERIA FOR GROUP WORK
   1. Are the procedures used in accordance with the techniques advocated in the program of education?
      a. What is the basis on which the groups are set up? (Common weaknesses, sociogram, etc.)
      b. Is the goal for each group set and understood?
      c. Have these goals been set by cooperative planning?
      d. In what type of activity is the group engaged - individual or group? Is there a free interplay of minds at all times?
      e. Are there evidences of evaluation within the group - by individuals and by the group?
      f. What is the extent and variety of materials used?
   2. Are there evidences of individual contributions by children in the group?

3. Are there evidences of committee work of children (charts, etc.)?
  4. Are there evidences of teacher-supervision of group procedures?
  5. Are there evidences of the growth of social skills, attitudes, and understandings of social living?
C. COMMITTEE WORK
  1. Group dynamics as a factor in committee work
     a. Sociograms and friendship charts
     b. Place of the "stars"
     c. Working the isolates into the committee
  2. As in grouping, the teacher starts with a single-committee and develops committee techniques with the members
  3. Selection of a chairman and a secretary by the committee - importance of leadership and followership
  4. Contributions of the members of a committee toward the solution of a problem - working together and all that it implies
  5. Place of the teacher
     a. She never "abdicates her position;" she advises and guides when indicated
     b. She watches closely those members with personal problems
     c. She anticipates difficulties in human relations
     d. She assigns a place for the committee to work comfortably
     e. She displays charts listing the committees, with leaders starred
     f. She makes available materials for research, including pictorial material and special materials for the non-reader or retarded reader
     g. She checks the progress of the group and of the individuals in the group regularly (before a reporting period, etc.)
  6. Standards for group work periods
     NOTE: These are suggestions for charts
     a. For a Group Leader
        a.1 Know what work to do each day
        a.2 Keep the group working
        a.3 Do not be too bossy
     b. For the Group
        b.1 We will speak softly
        b.2 We will talk only to our own group
        b.3 We will talk only about our own work
        b.4 We will try to find our own materials
        b.5 We will use our time wisely
        b.6 We will clean up when we have finished
     c. For Groups preparing a report
        c.1 Skim books for stories on the topic of your report
        c.2 Plan an outline of the whole topic
        c.3 Choose sub-topics for study
        c.4 Work on topics - make an outline, do some research, make something, etc.
        c.5 Give your report to the group for criticism
        c.6 Give the report to the class

IV. EVALUATION

A. ITEMS TO BE EVALUATED
  1. Mental development *(traditionally, this has been almost the sole emphasis)*
  2. Physical aspects

    3. Social aspects
    4. Emotional aspects
B. REASONS FOR EVALUATING
    1. It is a means of discovering group and individual growth
    2. It is a means of discovering whether children are developing at a rate commensurate with their general capacity (expectancy)
    3. To discover children's strengths and weaknesses, and necessity for specific help (diagnostic) in particular cases
    4. To indicate to the school how it can best provide the conditions of growth that make learning most economical and most effective
    5. Children learn more effectively when they take part in evaluation
        a. As members of a group, they learn to become aware of group needs (through learning they must acquire for a specific purpose)
        b. They learn how to plan for group needs (through practice in evaluating possible courses of action)
        c. They learn to take stock as they proceed with their tasks (through evaluating progress periodically)
        d. They learn ways of deciding when their project has reached a satisfactory conclusion (through practice in evaluating their achievements in the light of their original objectives)
C. WHEN TO EVALUATE
    1. It is a continuing activity, taking place at every stage of the learning process *(Evaluation is not concerned solely with end products)*
    2. The teacher evaluates situations as they occur
    3. "The quality of living" that goes on in a classroom is evaluated as an indication of class morale
    4. The amount of communication that takes place is, at all times, a significant evaluative factor
    5. The need for recording social adjustments, emotional maturity, attention span, language development, interests, and enthusiasms of children makes continuous evaluation a necessity
    6. Check lists and anecdotal records may be used to record what is observed
D. WHO EVALUATES?
    1. Everyone concerned in the educative process should take part in evaluation
        a. The children, with or without the guidance of the teacher, make valid judgments
        b. The teacher evaluates herself, the effectiveness of her procedures, the progress of her class and the individuals therein, the climate of her room, and the classroom situation
        c. The school, as a composite of teachers and supervisors, evaluates its curriculum, its services to children, its growth of teachers and supervisors, and its relationship to the life of the community
        d. Members of the community, especially parents, evaluate the school, its program and its teachers (The school should provide such information so as to make possible an intelligent evaluation on the community's part)
E. EVALUATION IN A UNIT OF WORK
    1. The unit should be evaluated in light of its objectives
    2. The primary objective is not absorption of a mass of facts, but the development of attitudes, understandings, and appreciations

3. The evaluation of desirable social relationships, the development of good habits of work and thought, and the imparting of basic concepts are our major social studies goals
4. Measurement of the so-called intangibles, while admittedly difficult, is possible (Formal tests, such as the California Tests of Personality and Winnetka Behavior Rating Scale are not so valuable as teacher observation and judgment)
5. The teacher, by recording objectively significant behavior, can observe the developmental pattern of growth in chidren (anecdotal records, etc.)
6. Teacher-made checklists and tests are helpful in determining growth and progress
   a. Tests in ascertaining places where information is available (A test of this type may be administered before and after a unit is taken. Growth may be measured by comparing results)
      a.1 Whom would you ask where to find a certain building if you were downtown?
      a.2 How would you locate a certain book if you were in the library?
      a.3 If you weren't sure whether a word ended in "ant" or "ent," how could you find out?
      a.4 Where would you look to find out something about an explorer?
      a.5 How could you tell, by looking at a map, whether New York is closer to Connecticut than it is to Virginia?
   b. Tests involving the relevancy of data to particular problems and tests involving the relevancy of statements to a conclusion
      b.1 Does a person's race or religion have any bearing on his athletic or musical ability?
      b.2 Since your city uses great amounts of food, does that mean that your city produces huge amounts of meat, grain, etc.?
   c. Tests involving the reliability of various sources, the matching of persons with the fields of their probable competence
      c.1 Would Mickey Mantle necessarily be an authority on international relations?
   d. Checklists of instances of voluntary cooperation (Does the child of his own accord clean up the area around his seat? Does the child bring materials from home?, etc.)
7. Methods of evaluation of a unit
   a. Objective tests *(prepared by teachers and pupils)*
   b. Teacher's written accounts and criticisms
   c. Teacher's anecdotal reports on individual and group work
   d. Matching achievement against predetermined objectives
   e. Comparison of activities and skills of this unit with those of preceding units
   f. Noting observations made by parents and community
8. Children's evaluation in a unit
   a. Charts: "Did I Do a Good Job?",etc.
   b. Evaluation "envelopes," in which children retain samples of their work and note-progress
   c. Children (and teacher) appraise:
      c.1 What have we learned?
      c.2 What should we remember?
      c.3 Did we do everything we set out to do?
      c.4 What must still be done?

c.5 What could we have done better?
c.6 What questions should be included on a "test of all the important things we learned?"
c.7 How can we make further use of the things we learned?
9. Evaluation is a means of discovering:
   a. Group and individual growth
   b. Teacher-effectiveness or weakness
   c. Group needs
   d. Curriculum strengths or deficiencies
   e. Objectives realized
   f. Experience gained
   g. Subject matter acquired
   h. Skills mastered
   i. Evidences of creative expression
   j. Evidences of growth toward desirable habits, attitudes, and appreciations
   k. Activities not yet completed
   l. Subject matter not covered

V. DISCIPLINE

A. MEANING
   1. Broad Meaning - The attainment by the individual of such knowledges, skills, habits, and attitudes as will promote the well-being of himself and of his social group.
   2. Narrow Meaning - The creation of classroom conditions to provide a wholesome environment for the best functioning of the individual and the group.
B. DISCIPLINE VS. ORDER
   1. Difference
      a. Discipline: Based on self-direction; maintained by building habits of self-control and by stressing the social need for desirable conduct. It aims at a self-directed class that works quietly and efficiently even though the teacher is temporarily too busy to supervise the class.
      b. Order: Based on instant obedience to commands emanating from above; depends on the teacher's ability to exercise constant surveillance and to use the pupils' fear of detection as a deterrent to undesirable action. Order reaches its height when the teacher can make the meaningless boast that she "can hear a pin drop."
   2. As a means toward discipline, order is sometimes essential. It may be a legitimate aid to discipline. As a goal in itself, it has little justification.
C. THE DIFFERENCE BETWEEN CONDUCT AND BEHAVIOR
   1. Conduct: The adult's reaction to the child's acts. It is considered "good" or "bad." Depends on adult's standards or values.
   2. Behavior: The child's reaction to stimuli (physical, mental, or social). It is "normal" or "abnormal." Depends on child's personality.
D. PLANES OF DISCIPLINE
   1. Obedience - military concept
   2. Personal domination by the teacher - "good order" concept
   3. Social pressure - living and working with others
   4. Self-discipline - living and working alone

E. GENERAL PRINCIPLES OF CLASSROOM DISCIPLINE
  1. Self-control is achieved through proper habit formation (psychological principles)
  2. Desirable discipline is social control within the school group
  3. Discipline should be positive and constructive, rather than negative and destructive
  4. It should appeal to the highest motives of which the pupil is capable
  5. It should impress pupils as being fair, reasonable, and socially necessary
F. POSITIVE VS. NEGATIVE DISCIPLINE
  1. The essential difference is one of attitude and approach
     a. Present conformity to rule vs. cultivating motives for sound action in later years
     b. Getting children to do the right thing vs. preventing them from doing the wrong thing
  2. Examples:

POSITIVE	NEGATIVE
a. Stimulating attention.	a. Coping with inattention. Scolding.
b. Creating desire to come to school because of meaningful activities.	b. Devising measures to curb truancy. Scolding.
c. Encouraging children to come early by starting promptly with interesting work and duties.	c. Devising new procedures to curb lateness. Scolding.
d. Awakening the desire to do things for the good of the school.	d. Compelling observance of class and school rules. Punishment.
e. Giving children opportunities of participating in class and school administration.	e. Teacher does everything. Doing things for children which they can be trained to do for themselves.

  3. Caution: It is impossible to dispense with negative discipline entirely, but the emphasis should be placed on the positive plane.
G. WHY SOME TEACHERS HAVE DISCIPLINARY TROUBLES
  1. Pedagogical Reasons
     a. Failure to employ appropriate subject matter and materials
     b. Poor teaching techniques
     c. Failure to consider the individual pupil's capacities, talents, and interests
  2. Classroom Management
     a. Failure to mechanize routines
     b. Unattractive, physically uncomfortable surroundings
  3. Personality
     a. Lack of tact   b. High strung manner
     c. Idiosyncrasies in dress   d. High pitched voice
     e. Lack of a sense of humor
  4. Psychological
     a. Lack of sympathy with children
     b. Procrastination in handling cases (not facing the issue)
     c. Lack of a fair disciplinary policy
H. CLASS MORALE AS A FACTOR IN CLASSROOM DISCIPLINE
  1. Meaning of morale or class spirit

      a. "Morale is the feeling among members of a group that stimulates them to work happily together toward the realization of shared aims"
      b. "The personality of the group born of common attitudes"
  2. How Developed
  L   a. *Leadership* of the teacher - she sets the tone
        a.1 Her personality - ability to fire others with enthusiasm for ideals and service; to arouse faith of pupils in her
        a.2 Her educational qualifications
        a.3 Her understanding of children
  A   b. Stressing of strong social *attitudes* - work of the group more important than that of the individual - team work of pupils
  C   c. Situations arousing *common* loyalties - participation in joint efforts
        c.1 Class projects - making things for the class or the school (posters, art objects, Christmas gifts to soldiers or destitute children, class newspaper, class party, help with parents' bazaar)
        c.2 Assembly programs, pageants
        c.3 Athletic teams
        c.4 Friendly competition with other classes (attendance records, contributions to the Red Cross)
  P   d. Situations arousing *pride* as a result of achievement and recognition
        d.1 Service to the class and school
        d.2 Records - attendance, punctuality, neatness, cleanliness, etc.
        d.3 Good deeds and accomplishments of classmates
        d.4 Accomplishment of learning goals (New Program)
  S   e. Attractive surroundings - contribution of pupils to the appearance of the room
        (Mnemonic - S C A L P)

I. THE USE OF INCENTIVES
  1. Distinction between incentives and motives
      a. Incentive - An environmental object or condition, the attainment or avoidance of which motivates behavior (external) - praise, blame, reward, punishment, rivalry
      b. Motive - The process within an organism which energizes or directs it toward a specific line of behavior (internal) - interest, need, urge, drive, desire
      c. Incentive is the stimulus; motive is the reaction, though the terms, including "motivation," are used loosely and interchangeably.
  2. Real vs. Artificial Motivation (intrinsic vs. extrinsic)
      a. Real Motivation - Gives purpose and direction to the learning process, is part of the task, arises from the value of the task for its own sake, is related to the life of the child (aroused by problems or challenges to which the child desires the answer or solution)
      b. Artificial Motivation - attempts to make uninteresting material attractive by sugarcoating; is based on traditional attitude that every lesson is a unit in itself; is usually unrelated or only slightly related to the task (stores, games, marks, rewards)

c. The new program vs. the traditional program from the point of view of motivation
   d. Some examples of real and artificial motivation:

REAL	ARTIFICIAL
1. Arithmetic: Learning percents through computing class averages in attendance or the standing of athletic teams	1. Learning by reference to father's bank account
2. Spelling: Learning words by writing a real letter	2. Learning through the desire to get a better mark
3. Geography: Learning the geography of the city through trips and excursions	3. Learning in order to do well on a quiz
4. Science: Learning about plants through growing them	4. Learning through a reference to the flower shop around the corner or to a picture
5. Social Studies: Learning the industries of a country through a study of how people live and work	5. Learning through reference to the work children's parents do
6. Art: Learning color and perspective through illustrating a unit by murals	6. Learning in order to get a good mark, to have work displayed, or to obtain the approval of the teacher

   (NOTE: *Extrinsic motivation is sometimes justifiable or desirable, but it should be subordinated to intrinsic drives wherever possible.*)
3. Incentives in the Classroom
   a. Principles
      a.1 The best incentive is one which makes a task significant to the child
      a.2 It should influence future as well as present actions and attitudes
      a.3 It should make doing an act a satisfying process
      a.4 It should encourage the social point of view
   b. Motives to which the teacher can appeal
      b.1 The desire to do the right for its own sake should always be the ultimate goal even with very young children
      b.2 The desire for self-respect - knowledge of progress, recognition of abilities or status
      b.3 The desire to win the approval of one's fellow - displaying good work, posting lists of children doing well, monitorships
      b.4 The desire to gain the approval of the teacher or one's parents - praise succeeds better than blame, recognizing the good better than scolding the bad, letters to parents
      b.5 The desire for new experiences - problems, excursions, class clubs, projects
      b.6 The desire to win a reward - need not be of material value - praise, exhibition of work, monitorships should be within reach of all - avoid bribery
(NOTE: *The lowest form of incentive is better than the best form of punishment.*)

J. CLASSROOM PUNISHMENTS
   1. The Basis for Punishment
      a. What should be the aim? Retributive, deterrent, or corrective?
      b. Punishment may be justified if it is *corrective*
         b.1 It must be a means of removing a tendency to unsocial behavior

b.2 It must not be a separate entity, but part of the education process
  b.3 It must aid in the process of adjusting behavior in a positive direction
 c. Criteria of effective punishment
  c.1 The child should be shown that he is being punished for a social transgression
  c.2 The teacher's personal feelings must not be a consideration
  c.3 Punishment is to be used only when the child fails to respond to incentives
  c.4 It should be adapted to the child (not uniform)
  c.5 It must not be unduly severe
  c.6 It must not leave a residue of antagonism or resentment
  c.7 It must not constitute the complete treatment for problem behavior
2. Punishment by Natural Consequence
 a. It is sound in theory but difficult in practice in the classroom (copying, cheating, failing to do work, obscene language)
 b. The principle can be followed, by making punishment seem to be a natural consequence wherever possible
3. Punishment by Fear
 a. Fear is an inhibiting rather than a stimulating force. It has a paralyzing harmful effect on development. It should rarely be used
 b. Corporal punishment is the lowest form of the use of fear. If ever administered, it should be for its shocking effect, rather than for punitive or corrective reasons
4. Evaluation of Classroom Punishments
 a. Minor punishments, such as staring at a child or calling his name - effective in nipping trouble in the bud
 b. Deprivation of position - effective if the door is held open for reinstatement
 c. Reprimands - effective, if given unemotionally and child is shown how his act interferes with others (must be used sparingly)
 d. Doing a written task - ineffective because it avoids the true causes of the trouble (I must come to school on time) and builds wrong associations (writing spelling words twenty five times)
 e. Picking up papers, etc. - effective if used as a means of making up for an offense, doing a positive deed in place of a negative
 f. Detention - generally ineffective because it leads to wrong associations with school
 g. Isolation - of doubtful value. The practice of having a child stand in a corner or in the corridor has no justification
 h. Social disapproval - effective if public humiliation does not result
 i. Saturation - ineffective and dangerous (it may backfire)
 j. Sarcasm - dangerous because mistaken for humor, builds resentment instead of cooperation (of doubtful value even with "smart alecks")
 k. Epithets - unjustified
 l. Sending for parent - effective if designed to understand causes and to devise program for cooperation between home and school

K. SOME PRACTICAL SUGGESTIONS FOR TEACHERS (*CHARACTERISTIC OF TRANSITION FROM ORDER TO DISCIPLINE*)
  1. Give pupils the impression that you expect perfect order
  2. Learn the names of all pupils as soon as possible
  3. Give no unnecessary orders or directions - no repetitions
  4. An explanatory statement, preparatory to giving a direction or order, reduces the possibility of confusion or disobedience
  5. Insist upon a reasonable compliance with those directions which are given
  6. Don't let little things go (*Nip disorder in the bud*)
  7. Keep the machinery of class management simple
  8. Plan lessons and all work well
  9. Keep the class busy on worthwhile work and activities
  10. Use rewards and punishments judiciously - watch for and reward desirable actions
  11. Avoid punishing in anger (It's the child, not the offense, that must be considered)
  12. Don't punish the group for the offense of an individual
  13. Don't make threats
  14. Severe penalties should not be used for minor offenses
  15. The teacher should never give the impression that she has exhausted her supply of punishments or rewards
  16. Avoid forcing an issue with a disobedient pupil before the class
  17. When a child is punished, keep the door open for him to return to the good graces of the class and the teacher
  18. Have a sense of humor
  19. Be fair and consistent in your decisions
  20. Have an element of surprise - something new - in class work
  21. Seat pupils so that opportunities for infraction are lessened
  22. The voice should be subdued, but audible enough to be heard clearly throughout the room
  23. Primarily, the handling of discipline cases is the responsibility of the teacher
  24. In handling discipline cases, the teacher may have reasonable recourse to the parents
  25. When a teacher has exhausted her own resources, or in the cases of emergency, she should call upon the supervisor for help

VI. BASIC FUNDAMENTALS OF EDUCATIONAL PSYCHOLOGY

A. CONDITIONING
   Learning takes place as a result of experience with outside stimuli. Responses are established by means of fixed associations.
   1. Principles of Conditioning (*for use by teachers*)
      a. Learners' responses must be systematically studied
      b. Records of progress indicate need for change of pace, concentration on difficult parts, return to basic skills, new motivation, variations in use of cues
      c. Learner should make own records of progress
      d. Unlearning takes place rapidly; support and repeated reinforcement are required to consolidate and maintain habitual performance
      e. Teacher must control stimulating conditions (motivation)
      f. Teacher must help learner by providing varying conditions and extended practice
      g. Forced pacing methods are a poor substitute for adequate motivation

B. LEARNING BY TRIAL AND ERROR (CONNECTIONISM)
   Learning involves the making of new mental and neural connections and the discarding or strengthening of old connections.
   1. Concerned with what takes place between S-R to the neural connections
      a. Atomistic analysis of behavior
      b. Development is from hereditary instincts and reflexes to acquired habits
      c. Intellect and intelligence are quantitative
   2. Thorndike's Laws of Learning
      a. Readiness - When a conduction unit is ready to act, conduction by it is satisfying and failure to conduct or being forced when not ready is annoying.
      b. Exercise - (Use and Disuse) Repetition with satisfaction strengthens the connection; disuse weakens the connection.
      c. Effect - Satisfaction strengthens the connection which it follows and to which it belongs. *(Importance of motivation)*
   3. Thorndike's Five Characteristics of Learning
      a. Multiple responses to the same external situation pervade nine tenths of learning.
      b. The responses made are the product of the "set" or "attitude" of the learner. The satisfaction or annoyance produced by a response is conditioned by the learner's attitude.
      c. Partial Activity: One or another element in the situation may be prepotent in determining the response.
      d. Law of Assimilation or Analogy: If one element in the situation resembles another, it will call forth a corresponding response.
      e. Associative Shifting - Omitting elements of a situation and still getting the same response. *(Conditioned response)*
   4. The Significance of "Cues" in Learning
      a. The learner tends to respond to loud sound, intense, brilliant or rapidly changing cues.
      b. Conspicuous stimuli may receive undue attention. Important stimuli may thus be overlooked.
      c. Cues help emphasize important stimuli.
      d. The teacher must discover when to use proper cues, and how much guidance to give the learner.
C. LEARNING BY INSIGHT: GESTALT PSYCHOLOGY
   1. Constant striving to make sense out of a situation
   2. The learner's efforts are not purely random
   3. Understanding is enhanced by responding to total patterns, to relation between things
   4. Motivation helps create perception of the problem
   5. The learner's background of experience aids in insight, in perceiving figurations, in seeing the relationships of the parts to the whole, and in acquiring meaning and value
D. THE FIELD THEORY (ORGANISMIC, HOLISTIC THEORY)
   1. Derived from the Gestalt theory
   2. Insight is the alteration of organic structure within an area of the "whole organism"
   3. Significances
      a. Breakdown of atomistic views
      b. Importance of chemical function of neural mechanisms
      c. Fundamental role of "feelings and emotions" in learning

      d. Muscular coordination of the complete organism is a factor in skill acquisition
      e. Recognition of the principle of maturation
      f. Best motivation derives from needs of learners

E. TRANSFER OF TRAINING
  1. Recognized as significant in educational theory and practice
     a. Traditional Concept - Doctrine of Formal Discipline: the mind gains strength through use, and this strength is automatically available in all situations. (Faculties of the Mind)
     b. Current Concept - No faculties as such. Transfer is a fact of mental life occurring under certain mental conditions, not because of external causes.
  2. Factors Influencing Transfer
     a. Methods of procedure in learning and teaching
     b. Attitude of readiness set up by instructions given
     c. Degree of mastery of the material learned
     d. Integration of the initial learning - as to content and method
     e. Extent to which generalization and application are applied - "psychological organization"
  3. Current Theories of Transfer
     a. Theory of Identical Elements (Thorndike)
        a.1 Identity of content
        a.2 Identity of procedure
        a.3 Identity of aims or ideals
        These identical elements make use of the same neural bonds.
     b. Theory of Generalization or Abstraction or Relationship
        Transfer takes place to the extent that one generalizes his experiences and is able to apply general principles to different situations. (Scientific method)
  4. Implications for the Supervisor
     a. Materials used should have real value for children, not for mental discipline.
     b. A subject which has slight transfer value in a large field may be of more value than a subject which has a greater transfer value, but in a very limited field.
     c. The difficulty of a subject is not any indication of its transfer value.
     d. Recognition of child growth and development is the basic aim.
     e. The position accorded any subject in the school curriculum should be decided by the value of the special training it affords and by the social significance of its content rather than by its promise to develop general intellectual capacities.
  5. Implications for the Teacher
     a. The most effective use of knowledge is assured, not through acquisition of any particular item of experience but only through the establishment of associations which give it general value.
     b. Transfer is most common at the higher levels of intellectual activity.
     c. Children should receive training in methods of memorizing, acquiring skills, and in solving problems.
     d. If transfer value is slight, then it is most economical to practice directly those habits and skills we wish to develop.
     e. An individual's ability to apply knowledge is not in proportion to his knowledge of facts.

  f. The teacher should know what it is that she wants the children to transfer to other fields, and she must learn by experience or experiment how to teach for transfer.
  g. The theory of transfer is recognized by all schools of psychology. More research is necessary before teachers can be guided by the theory to any great extent.
F. HABIT
 1. Meaning - A learned response made automatically to the appropriate stimulus.
 2. Principles of Habit Formation (Bagley)
  a. Focalize consciousness (Motivation)
   a.1 Give clearest possible idea of habit to be formed
   a.2 Use demonstration a.3 Make it vivid
   a.4 Arouse motivation
   a.5 Give instruction in how habits are formed
   a.6 Multiple sense appeal
  b. Attentive repetition
   b.1 Vigorous, short, definite drill b.2 Use devices
   b.3 Have a definite goal (focalization)
   b.4 Watch for lag in attention
   b.5 Vary the number of repetitions
   b.6 "Practice makes perfect" only if with attention
  c. No exceptions
   c.1 Analyze habit in advance to prepare for likely slips
   c.2 Give special drill on difficult parts
   c.3 Put child on his guard c.4 Remove opposing stimuli
   c.5 Avoid forming similar habits at the same time
   c.6 Punishment, if necessary, should follow wrong act
  d. Automatization
   d.1 Attention to weak elements
   d.2 Distribution of practice (optional length)
 3. Values and Limitations
  a. Diminishes fatigue because habit mechanizes reactions so that they accomplish their function with directness and minimum time and effort
  b. Releases consciousness for the guidance of other activities
  c. Makes responses reliable and accurate
  d. Complete domination, however, retards progress
  e. Sensibilities often deadened, lessening normal emotional tones
  f. Difficult to break bad habits
 4. Breaking Bad Habits
  a. Avoid the situation which will result in the undesirable habit
  b. Avoid opportunity for its practice
  c. Concentrate on one or two bad habits at a time
  d. Follow the principles of habit formation for developing the reverse of the bad habit (Substitution)
  e. Attach unpleasant feeling tone
 5. Significance for Teaching
  a. Dependence of habit on sensory stimulation *(Habits never initiate themselves)*
  b. Importance of gradation of subject matter to develop mechanical habits
  c. In skills, improvement is very rapid at first
  d. Attention to physical and psychical conditions (time of day, length of period, etc.)

      d. Muscular coordination of the complete organism is a factor in skill acquisition
      e. Recognition of the principle of maturation
      f. Best motivation derives from needs of learners

E. TRANSFER OF TRAINING
   1. Recognized as significant in educational theory and practice
      a. Traditional Concept - Doctrine of Formal Discipline: the mind gains strength through use, and this strength is automatically available in all situations. (Faculties of the Mind)
      b. Current Concept - No faculties as such. Transfer is a fact of mental life occurring under certain mental conditions, not because of external causes.
   2. Factors Influencing Transfer
      a. Methods of procedure in learning and teaching
      b. Attitude of readiness set up by instructions given
      c. Degree of mastery of the material learned
      d. Integration of the initial learning - as to content and method
      e. Extent to which generalization and application are applied - "psychological organization"
   3. Current Theories of Transfer
      a. Theory of Identical Elements (Thorndike)
          a.1 Identity of content
          a.2 Identity of procedure
          a.3 Identity of aims or ideals
         These identical elements make use of the same neural bonds.
      b. Theory of Generalization or Abstraction or Relationship Transfer takes place to the extent that one generalizes his experiences and is able to apply general principles to different situations. (Scientific method)
   4. Implications for the Supervisor
      a. Materials used should have real value for children, not for mental discipline.
      b. A subject which has slight transfer value in a large field may be of more value than a subject which has a greater transfer value, but in a very limited field.
      c. The difficulty of a subject is not any indication of its transfer value.
      d. Recognition of child growth and development is the basic aim.
      e. The position accorded any subject in the school curriculum should be decided by the value of the special training it affords and by the social significance of its content rather than by its promise to develop general intellectual capacities.
   5. Implications for the Teacher
      a. The most effective use of knowledge is assured, not through acquisition of any particular item of experience but only through the establishment of associations which give it general value.
      b. Transfer is most common at the higher levels of intellectual activity.
      c. Children should receive training in methods of memorizing, acquiring skills, and in solving problems.
      d. If transfer value is slight, then it is most economical to practice directly those habits and skills we wish to develop.
      e. An individual's ability to apply knowledge is not in proportion to his knowledge of facts.

  f. The teacher should know what it is that she wants the children to transfer to other fields, and she must learn by experience or experiment how to teach for transfer.
  g. The theory of transfer is recognized by all schools of psychology. More research is necessary before teachers can be guided by the theory to any great extent.
F. HABIT
 1. Meaning - A learned response made automatically to the appropriate stimulus.
 2. Principles of Habit Formation (Bagley)
  a. Focalize consciousness (Motivation)
   a.1 Give clearest possible idea of habit to be formed
   a.2 Use demonstration a.3 Make it vivid
   a.4 Arouse motivation
   a.5 Give instruction in how habits are formed
   a.6 Multiple sense appeal
  b. Attentive repetition
   b.1 Vigorous, short, definite drill b.2 Use devices
   b.3 Have a definite goal (focalization)
   b.4 Watch for lag in attention
   b.5 Vary the number of repetitions
   b.6 "Practice makes perfect" only if with attention
  c. No exceptions
   c.1 Analyze habit in advance to prepare for likely slips
   c.2 Give special drill on difficult parts
   c.3 Put child on his guard c.4 Remove opposing stimuli
   c.5 Avoid forming similar habits at the same time
   c.6 Punishment, if necessary, should follow wrong act
  d. Automatization
   d.1 Attention to weak elements
   d.2 Distribution of practice (optional length)
 3. Values and Limitations
  a. Diminishes fatigue because habit mechanizes reactions so that they accomplish their function with directness and minimum time and effort
  b. Releases consciousness for the guidance of other activities
  c. Makes responses reliable and accurate
  d. Complete domination, however, retards progress
  e. Sensibilities often deadened, lessening normal emotional tones
  f. Difficult to break bad habits
 4. Breaking Bad Habits
  a. Avoid the situation which will result in the undesirable habit
  b. Avoid opportunity for its practice
  c. Concentrate on one or two bad habits at a time
  d. Follow the principles of habit formation for developing the reverse of the bad habit (Substitution)
  e. Attach unpleasant feeling tone
 5. Significance for Teaching
  a. Dependence of habit on sensory stimulation *(Habits never initiate themselves)*
  b. Importance of gradation of subject matter to develop mechanical habits
  c. In skills, improvement is very rapid at first
  d. Attention to physical and psychical conditions (time of day, length of period, etc.)

     e. Recognition of possible periods of lapse and plateau
        e. 1 Need for rest
        e. 2 Attention and interest misdirected
        e. 3 Conflict in habits
        e. 4 Minor causes - indisposition, irritation
     f. Recognition of individual differences in habit formation
     g. Rate of forgetting high at first
     h. Consideration of Speed vs. Accuracy
     i. Recognition of three sets of habits (Mechanical;Subject Matter; Mental)

G. INDIVIDUAL DIFFERENCES
  1. Principles
     a. Pupils differ in degree of ability, not in the ability itself
     b. Individuals differ in degree of difficulty of tasks which they can learn; also in the method of learning
     c. Pupils of the same age and grade differ greatly - there is considerable overlapping of successive grades
     d. No one class can ever be entirely homogeneous - variations are continuous
     e. There are no readily available and fixed categories which the school can employ for the purpose of differentiated instruction
     f. Provision for individualization presents teaching and administrative difficulties
     g. Chronological age alone cannot be the determinant of an individual's capacity
  2. Conclusions for the School
     a. Administrative
        a. 1 Vary the time element
        a. 2 Flexible grouping
        a. 3 Testing programs
        a. 4 Modification of the curriculum
        a. 5 Provision for educational guidance
        a. 6 Flexible promotions
        a. 7 Supervision of proper teaching practices
     b. Curricular
        b. 1 Individualization of instruction
        b. 2 Diagnostic testing and remedial teaching
        b. 3 Provision for individual methods of learning
        b. 4 Grouping within the class
        b. 5 Record of needs, progress, and evaluation

VII. HISTORY OF EDUCATION

A. LEADERS
  1. Socrates (5th century B.C.)(469-399 B.C.)(Athens, Period of Sophists)
     (1) Writings - Left no writings, is studied in works of Plato and Xenophon.
     (2) Emphasis - Highest formulation of principles of moral life up to his time.
     (3) Contributions - His starting point: "Man is the measure of all things" (Protagoras).
     (4) Developed opinion into true or universal knowledge.
     (5) Aid of education: Not sophist brilliancy of speech, but knowledge arising from power of thought, analysis of experience.
     (6) Method: Dialectic, skillful questioning, distinguishing between permanent form and changing appearance, forming concepts from percepts.

2. Plato (4th century B.C.) (429-348 B.C.) (Athens, Academy)
   (1) Writings - "Republic," "Dialogues."
   (2) Three social classes: philosophers, warriors, workers.
   (3) Six major concerns of life: psychology, knowledge, soul, state, politics, ethics.
   (4) The ideal *State*, which exists for the realization of *justice*, consists of three classes of people: philosophers, soldiers, and workers.
   These classes of society correspond to the soul (or *psychology* of the individual: intelligence or reason; the passions, spiri or will; and the desires, appetites, or sensations.
   The *ethics* of the classes embraces the traits of character whi they should exhibit: wisdom, or correctness of thought; honor, courage, energy of will, or justice of the heart; and temperan self-control, or justice of the senses.
   Politics indicates the duties of the classes: the philosophers are to rule, the soldiers to protect and defend the State, and the workers to obey and support those above them.
   (5) Aim of education: To discover and develop individual qualifica tions to fit into classes of society; harmony of individual an social motives.
3. Aristotle (3rd century B.C.) (384-322 B.C.)(Athens, Lyceum)
   (1) Writings - "Organon," "Politics," "Ethics," "Metaphysics."
   (2) Like Plato, he believed the highest art of man to be to direct society so as to produce the greatest good for mankind.
   (3) Education is subject to politics, each kind of state having it appropriate kind of education.
   (4) Education is a life activity.
   (5) Method: Objective and scientific; used inductive method, and thus founded practically all the modern sciences.
   (6) Education democratic, although all could not reach the same hi point.
   (7) Greatest systematizer of knowledge.
   (8) Formulated deductive reasoning; dialectic given form and unive sal influence.
   (9) Gave vocabulary of reasoning to the world.
4. Comenius (17th century) (1592-1670)
   (1) Writings - "Orbus Pictus," "Vestibulum,""Janua,""School of Infancy," "The Great Didactic"
   (2) Sense - realist
      a. The teacher should appeal through sense-perception to under stand the child
   (3) Contributions
      a. Forerunner of 18th and 19th century educational theory
      b. Reformed Latin textbooks
5. John Locke (17th century) (1632-1704)
   (1) Writings - "Essay on Conduct of the Human Understanding," "Thoughts"
   (2) Founder of modern psychology; advocate of faculty psychology
   (3) Empiricism; induction
   (4) Conception of the child's mind as a "tabula rasa" (blank slate
   (5) His influence strong up to the middle of the 19th century
6. Rousseau (18th century) (1712-1778)
   (1) Writings - "La Nouvelle Heloise," "Emile"
   (2) Education is life, not preparation for life
   (3) Importance of the child
   (4) Functional education
   (5) Individual differences

7. Johann Bernard Basedow (18th century)(1723-1790)
    (1) Writings -"Elementarwerk," "Book of Method"; established school called Philanthropinum, at Dessau.
    (2) Belongs to the line of Sense-Realists following Rousseau and forerunner to Pestalozzi.
    (3) Made first attempt since Comeniums to improve the work of the school through the use of appropriate textbooks.
    (4) Ideas embodied:
        (a) Children to be treated as such, not as adults.
        (b) Each child taught a handicraft for educational and social reasons.
        (c) Vernacular rather than classical languages chief subject matter of education.
        (d) Instruction connected with realities rather than with words.
        (e) Rich and poor educated together.
    (5) Contributions
        (a) Trained teachers.
        (b) Milder form of discipline.
        (c) Broader and more philanthropic view of man's duty to his fellow-man.
8. Pestalozzi (18th and early 19th century)(1746-1827)
    (1) Writings - "How Gertrude Teaches Her Children," "Leonard and Gertrude"
    (2) Sense impression
    (3) Respect for the individuality of the child
    (4) Discipline based upon love
    (5) Education for the subnormal
    (6) Normal schools
9. Herbart (19th and first half of the 19th century)(1776-1841)
    (1) Writings - First to write a textbook on psychology,"Testbook of Psychology"; Psychology as a Science"
    (2) Rejected the faculty psychology of Pestalozzi
    (3) Substituted his own method - the Five Formal Steps:
        (a) Preparation   (b) Presentation   (c) Comparison
        (d) Generalization (e) Application
    (4) Organization and technique of classroom instruction
    (5) Emphasis on environment in education
10. Froebel (first half of 19th century)(1782-1852)
    (1) Writings - "Education of Man," "Mutter," "Kose Lieder"
    (2) Founder of the kindergarten and the kindergarten idea
    (3) Education by doing
11. Spencer, Herbert (19th century) (1820-1903)
    (1) Writings - "Principles of Psychology," "Synthetic Philosophy," "Essays on Education"
    (2) Not originator but developer of the best in democratic education of his predecessors
    (3) Emphasis on scientific knowledge
12. Mann, Horace (19th century) (1796-1859)
    (1) Reference: Mary T.Mann, ed.,"The Life and Works of Horace Mann" (5 vols.-1891)
    (2) First secretary of the first Board of Education of Massachusetts (1817)
    (3) Conception of education as universal,secular,public,free, and compulsory
    (4) Outstanding organizer in education

13. Barnard, Henry (19th century) (1811-1900)
    (1) Writings - Edited "The American Journal of Education"(1855-18
    (2) Held positions in Connecticut and Rhode Island similar to tha
        of Horace Mann in Massachusetts, i.e., Secretary of the Board
        of Education in Connecticut, 1838-1842, 1851-1855; and State
        Superintendent of Education in Rhode Island, 1845-1849.
    (3) First United States Commissioner of Education 1867-1870
14. Dewey, John (19th and 20th century) (1859-1952)
    (1) Writings - "The School and Society," "Democracy and Education,"
        "Experience and Nature," "Freedom and Culture"
    (2) Education is life, not a preparation for life
    (3) Learning takes place by doing
    (4) The bases of education are psychological and sociological
    (5) Father of progressive education ("activity" program)

B. CONCEPTUALIZED DEFINITIONS AND AIMS OF EDUCATION
   1. Character, morality: Plutarch (Spartans), Herbart
   2. Perfect development: Plato, Rabelais, Montaigne, Comenius, Locke,
      Parker, Pestalozzi
   3. Happiness: Aristotle, James Mill
   4. Truth: Socrates
   5. Citizenship: Luther, Milton
   6. Mastery of nature: Bacon, Huxley
   7. Religion: Comenius
   8. Mental power, discipline: Locke, Van Dyke, Ruediger
   9. Preparation for the future: Kant
  10. Habits: Rousseau, William James
  11. Unfolding: Froebel, Hegel
  12. Holy life: Froebel
  13. Interests: Herbart
  14. Knowledge: L.F. Ward
  15. Complete living: Spencer
  16. Culture, liberal education: Dewey
  17. Skill: Nathaniel Butler, E.C. Moore
  18. Inheritance of culture: N.M. Butler
  19. Socialization: W.T. Harris, Dewey
  20. Social efficiency: Dewey, Bagley
  21. Adjustment: Dewey, Ruediger, Chapman and Counts
  22. Growth: Dewey
  23. Organization of experience: Dewey
  24. Self realization: Dewey and Tufts
  25. Satisfying wants: Thorndike and Gates
  26. Insight: Gentile

ANSWER SHEET

TEST NO. _____ PART _____ TITLE OF POSITION _____
(AS GIVEN IN EXAMINATION ANNOUNCEMENT - INCLUDE OPTION, IF ANY)

PLACE OF EXAMINATION _____ DATE _____
(CITY OR TOWN)   (STATE)

RATING

USE THE SPECIAL PENCIL. MAKE GLOSSY BLACK MARKS.

Make only ONE mark for each answer. Additional and stray marks may be counted as mistakes. In making corrections, erase errors COMPLETELY.

ANSWER SHEET

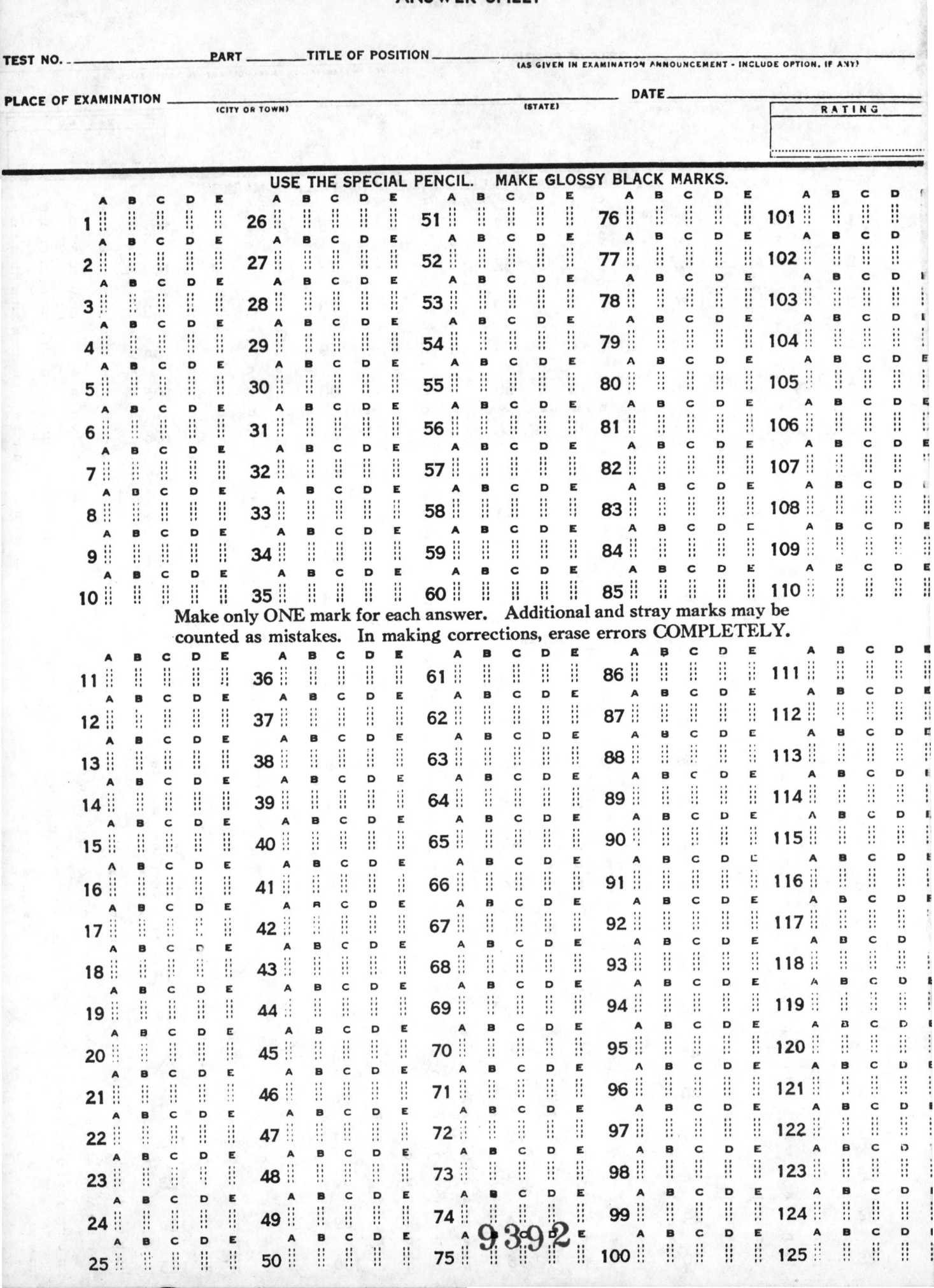

TEST NO. _____ PART _____ TITLE OF POSITION _____ (AS GIVEN IN EXAMINATION ANNOUNCEMENT - INCLUDE OPTION, IF ANY)

PLACE OF EXAMINATION _____ (CITY OR TOWN) _____ (STATE) _____ DATE _____

RATING

USE THE SPECIAL PENCIL. MAKE GLOSSY BLACK MARKS.

Make only ONE mark for each answer. Additional and stray marks may be counted as mistakes. In making corrections, erase errors COMPLETELY.

9392